DOLOMITES TRAVEL GUIDE 2023

The Ultimate Guide to Discover the Top Attractions, Activities, Where to Stay, Dine, Culture and Plan your trip to Italy's Alpine Gem. Your Complete Blueprint for an Unforgettable Journey to Dolomite.

Lisa T. Morris

Copyright 2023 by Lisa T. Morris

All rights reserved. No part of this book may be reproduced, distributed, or transmitted in any form or by any means, including photocopying, recording, or other electronic or mechanical methods, without the prior written permission of the publisher, except in the case of brief quotations embodied in critical reviews and specific other noncommercial uses permitted by copyright law

TABLE OF CONTENTS

INTRODUCTION.. **5**

CHAPTER 1:
GETTING TO KNOW THE DOLOMITES...... **10**
    Why Visit the Dolomites?.................................. 10
    Geography and Climate of the Dolomites.......... 14
    Brief History & Culture... 18

CHAPTER 2:
PLANNING YOUR TRIP............................. **22**
    Best Time to Visit Dolomites............................. 22
    How to Get to Dolomites.................................... 27
    Getting Around in the Dolomites 32
    Visa and Travel Requirements......................... 37
    What to Pack for Your Dolomites Trip.............. 41
    Reliable Places to Book Your Trip to the
    Dolomites..46

CHAPTER 3:
WHERE TO STAY AND DINE..................... **50**
    Accommodation Options in the Dolomites &
    Recommendations... 52
    Hotels and Resorts:... 52
    Bed and Breakfasts (B&Bs):............................. 53
    Mountain Huts and Lodges:............................. 54
    Camping and RV Options:................................ 56
    Unique Accommodation Experiences:............. 57
    Dining and Michelin-Starred Restaurants........ 59
    Local Cuisine and Must-Try Dishes.................. 63

CHAPTER 4: EXPLORING THE DOLOMITES...................69

   Major Cities And Towns....................................... 69
   Natural Wonders and Landmarks......................79
   Historic Sites and Museums...............................85
   Wildlife and Nature Reserves............................ 88

CHAPTER 5
OUTDOOR ACTIVITIES IN THE DOLOMITES 92

   Hiking and Trekking trails................................. 93
   Mountain Biking Routes..................................... 96
   Rock Climbing Adventures.................................99
   Adventure Sports... 102

CHAPTER 6:
EXPERIENCING DOLOMITES CULTURE 104

   Arts, Crafts, and Artisans...................................104
   Dolomite's Festivals and Events.......................108
   Folklore and Local Legends.............................. 112
   Discover Popular Shopping Destinations......... 116
   Cultural Etiquette and Customs........................120

CHAPTER 7:
BEYOND THE DOLOMITES...................... 124

   Day Trips and Excursions.................................124
   Exploring Nearby Regions................................129
   Hidden Gems and Lesser-Known Spots...........133

CHAPTER 8: VISITING THE DOLOMITES ON A BUDGET 138
- Budget Accommodation Options 139
- Affordable Dining Options 143
- Free or Low-Cost Attractions 146
- Transportation Savings 149
- Money- saving Tips 152

CHAPTER 9: DURATION AND ITINERARY SUGGESTIONS 156
- Short stay 3-Days Dolomites Itinerary 156
- 7-Days Dolomites Itinerary 160
- Family- Friendly Activities Itinerary 164
- Romantic Retreats and Honeymoon Escapes .. 167

CHAPTER 10: PRACTICAL TIPS AND SAFETY 170
- Health and Safety 170
- Travel Insurance 172
- Language and Communication 175
- Useful Italian Phrases 178
- Money and Currency Exchange 180

CHAPTER 11: RESOURCES AND HELPFUL INFORMATION 183
- Emergency Contacts 183
- Local Tourism Offices and Contacts 186
- Recommended Tour Operators 189
- Useful Websites, Maps, Apps 192

Conclusion 196

INTRODUCTION

Welcome to the Dolomites, a mesmerizing Alpine wonderland that captivates the soul with its breathtaking beauty and enchanting landscapes. As the author of this travel guide, I am thrilled to share with you my personal journey to the Dolomites and provide you with a comprehensive and engaging companion for your own adventure to this awe-inspiring destination.

My fascination with the Dolomites began long before I set foot on its storied terrain. I had heard tales of its dramatic peaks, vibrant meadows, and ethereal alpenglow, and these stories ignited an insatiable wanderlust within me. In the summer of 2022, I embarked on a soul-stirring journey to the heart of the Dolomites, and little did I know that this trip would forever leave an indelible mark on my heart.

As I arrived in the charming town of Cortina d'Ampezzo, I was immediately welcomed by the warm embrace of the majestic mountains that surrounded me. The Dolomites, a UNESCO World Heritage Site, are truly a geological masterpiece, with their unique rock formations painted in hues of pink and gold by the setting sun. The sheer grandeur of this Alpine paradise was beyond words, and I felt a profound connection with nature that I had never experienced before.

Throughout my journey, I wandered along alpine trails adorned with wildflowers, stood in awe of mighty waterfalls cascading down ancient cliffs, and encountered the friendly locals who welcomed me with genuine hospitality. The Dolomites offered an array of outdoor adventures, from exhilarating hikes and thrilling rock climbing to serene moments of reflection by serene lakes.

In this travel guide, I aim to impart not only practical information but also the personal experiences and insights gained during my own expedition. I believe that the heart of any journey lies not just in the destinations visited, but in the stories we collect along the way.

Let this guide be your trusted companion as you navigate the charming towns and hidden valleys of the Dolomites. From planning your trip, choosing the perfect accommodations, to uncovering the region's cultural treasures, I've curated every section with care, ensuring that you have the most fulfilling and unforgettable experience possible.

Whether you're an intrepid adventurer seeking the thrill of the mountains, a family looking for a fun-filled vacation, a couple seeking a romantic escape, or a nature enthusiast eager to immerse yourself in the region's rich biodiversity, the Dolomites have something extraordinary to offer every traveler, all year round. Let your senses be captivated by the beauty of this alpine paradise, and allow yourself to be enchanted by its charm.

As you turn the pages of this guide, I hope you feel the same sense of wonder and excitement that I felt during my own expedition. May it inspire you to create your own cherished memories, forge new connections with the world around you, and uncover the hidden gems that make the Dolomites an unrivaled destination.

So without further delay, let's start on this adventure together. From the pages of this travel guide to the stunning landscapes that await you, may your Trip to the Dolomites be nothing short of extraordinary. Prepare to be captivated, inspired, and forever changed by this unparalleled alpine paradise.

Before we delve into the practical aspects of planning your trip, let me share with you the captivating beauty that lies in the heart of the Dolomites. The region boasts breathtaking vistas and picturesque valleys that are sure to leave you awe-inspired. The Dolomites are renowned for their mountainous landscapes, and as you traverse their high-altitude terrains, you'll be enchanted by the natural wonders that surround you.

CHAPTER 1: GETTING TO KNOW THE DOLOMITES

Why Visit the Dolomites?

There are few places on Earth that possess the awe-inspiring beauty and captivating charm of the Dolomites. As I reflect on my own journey to this enchanting Alpine wonderland, I can confidently say that the question should not be, "Why visit Dolomite?" but rather, "Why wouldn't you?"

Here are the reasons..

1. Majestic Alpine Landscape:

The Dolomites boast a landscape that seems plucked straight from a fairytale. Towering peaks, majestic cliffs, and pristine valleys create an otherworldly panorama that leaves visitors in absolute wonder. As the first rays of sunlight touch the rocky spires, casting a warm rosy glow, the enchanting phenomenon known as the "Enrosadira" bathes the mountains in a surreal kaleidoscope of colors - an experience that is truly unparalleled.

2. Outdoor Paradise:

For nature enthusiasts and adventure seekers alike, the Dolomites offer an array of outdoor activities that cater to every passion and skill level. Whether you're an avid hiker yearning to conquer challenging trails, a mountain biker seeking thrilling descents, or a rock climber dreaming of scaling the iconic faces, the Dolomites deliver an exhilarating playground for all.

3. UNESCO World Heritage Site:

Designated as a UNESCO World Heritage Site in 2009, the Dolomites hold significant cultural and geological importance. The region's unique geology, with its dolomite rock formations, bears witness to millions of years of Earth's history. The preservation of its natural heritage ensures that future generations can continue to marvel at its splendor.

4. Rich Cultural Heritage:

Beyond its natural beauty, the Dolomites boast a rich cultural heritage deeply rooted in the Alpine way of life. Traditional mountain villages exude a sense of timelessness, and the locals' warm hospitality and preserved customs create an authentic and welcoming atmosphere. Immerse yourself in the region's history, folklore, and delicious cuisine to truly connect with the soul of the Dolomites.

5. Year-Round Destination:

Unlike many mountainous regions that cater to either winter or summer activities, the Dolomites are a year-round destination. Each season brings its own enchantment and opportunities. From skiing and snowboarding in winter to hiking and cycling in summer, the Dolomites offer endless possibilities for exploration and adventure, regardless of the time of year.

6. Unforgettable Experiences:
In the Dolomites, every step, every turn, and every view presents an opportunity for an unforgettable experience. Whether it's witnessing a breathtaking sunrise from a mountain peak, savoring the simplicity of a picnic amidst wildflowers, or discovering hidden alpine lakes nestled in secluded valleys, the Dolomites promise moments that will linger in your heart forever.

As I look back on my own journey to the Dolomites, I can't help but be overwhelmed by a sense of gratitude for having experienced this breathtaking wonderland. The allure of the Dolomites lies not just in its scenic beauty but also in its ability to awaken the spirit of adventure, instill a profound appreciation for nature's wonders, and create lasting memories that transcend time

Geography and Climate of the Dolomites

As you begin your exploration of the Dolomites, it's essential to familiarize yourself with the region's geography and climate, for they play a pivotal role in shaping the breathtaking beauty and unique allure of this Alpine wonderland.

The Dolomites, also known as the "Pale Mountains," are a mountain range located in northeastern Italy, predominantly in the regions of South Tyrol, Trentino, and Veneto. This UNESCO World Heritage Site is a geological marvel, it covers an expansive area of approximately 141,903 hectares. distinguished by its striking rock formations, which glow in hues of pink, gold, and orange during sunrise and sunset.

The geological history of the Dolomites is what makes them truly unique. Composed predominantly of dolomite rock, these ancient mountains were formed over millions of years through a complex interplay of sedimentation, tectonic activity, and erosion. The result is a breathtaking landscape adorned with soaring peaks, dramatic cliffs, and distinct rock formations that give the range its characteristic pink and golden glow, especially during sunrise and sunset - a spectacle known as the "Enrosadira."

One of the defining features of the Dolomites is its abundance of awe-inspiring peaks, many of which soar over 3,000 meters above sea level. Among the most iconic are the Marmolada, the highest peak in the Dolomites and known as the "Queen of the Dolomites," and the Tre Cime di Lavaredo, a trio of dramatic and jagged rock formations that have become an emblem of the region.

Beyond its stunning landscapes, the Dolomites boast a rich and diverse ecosystem. The region is a sanctuary for a wide variety of flora and fauna, with rare alpine plants, such as edelweiss and gentians, dotting the meadows.

The Dolomites are also home to several picturesque valleys, where charming villages and towns are nestled amidst lush green meadows and towering peaks. Each valley boasts its own distinct character and cultural heritage, offering travelers a diverse range of experiences.

As for the climate, the Dolomites experience a mix of Mediterranean and Alpine influences. Summers are generally mild with average temperatures ranging from 15°C to 25°C (59°F to 77°F) in the valleys, making it an ideal time for hiking, biking, and exploring the region's rich flora and fauna. However, temperatures can be cooler at higher elevations, so it's essential to be prepared for varying weather conditions.

In contrast, winters in the Dolomites are a true wonderland for winter sports enthusiasts. The region transforms into a winter paradise, blanketed in snow, and offers a myriad of opportunities for skiing, snowboarding, snowshoeing, and more. The valleys are adorned with festive Christmas markets, and the charming villages exude a cozy and welcoming atmosphere.

It's important to note that the climate in the Dolomites can vary significantly depending on the altitude and the specific location within the region. As you ascend to higher elevations, temperatures tend to drop, and weather conditions can change rapidly. It's always advisable to check weather forecasts and be equipped with appropriate clothing and gear when exploring the mountains.

The unique geography and climate of the Dolomites not only contribute to its extraordinary beauty but also make it a year-round destination with a rich array of experiences for every type of traveler. Whether you visit in the summertime to witness the alpine meadows in bloom or in the winter to indulge in exhilarating snow sports, the Dolomites will undoubtedly leave an indelible impression on your heart

Brief History & Culture

The Dolomites have a rich and fascinating history that spans thousands of years, shaped by various civilizations and cultures that have called this region home. From ancient tribes to modern-day societies, the cultural heritage of the Dolomites reflects the resilience and deep connection between its people and the magnificent landscape they inhabit.

Historical Roots:
The earliest human presence in the Dolomites can be traced back to the Paleolithic era, with evidence of human activity found in caves and rock shelters. Throughout antiquity, the region was inhabited by various tribes, including the Rhaetians and the Celts, who left their mark on the landscape through artifacts, inscriptions, and burial sites.

The Romans also played a significant role in the region's history, leaving behind roads, bridges, and fortresses that attest to their influence. The strategic importance of the Dolomites as a crossing point between the Italian peninsula and central Europe made it a pivotal location for trade and military campaigns.

The Dolomites remained relatively untouched by outside influences until the Middle Ages, when feudal lords and bishops established their dominion over the valleys and mountain passes. The construction of castles and fortifications during this period was a testament to the turbulent times and territorial struggles that defined the region.

Cultural Diversity:
Today, the Dolomites are home to a diverse mix of cultures and languages, owing to its location at the crossroads of Italy, Austria, and Switzerland. The predominant languages spoken in the region are Italian, German, and Ladin, a Romance language spoken by the Ladin people, who have inhabited the area for centuries.

The Ladin culture is particularly distinct and is deeply rooted in the Dolomites' history. Its unique traditions, customs, and folklore have been passed down through generations, preserving a sense of identity and pride in their alpine heritage. From vibrant festivals celebrating local cuisine and music to intricately crafted traditional costumes, the Ladin culture adds an extra layer of richness to the Dolomite experience.

Architecture and Art:
Throughout the Dolomites, you'll find a blend of architectural styles that reflect the region's cultural diversity. Ancient churches and chapels adorned with frescoes stand alongside quaint mountain villages with wooden chalets, showcasing the fusion of religious influences and traditional mountain architecture.

The Dolomites have also inspired numerous artists, writers, and poets over the years. From famous painters capturing the breathtaking landscapes on canvas to literary works that immortalize the region's beauty and charm, the arts have played an essential role in capturing the essence of the Dolomites.

Preservation and Conservation:

In recognition of its outstanding cultural and natural value, the Dolomites were designated a UNESCO World Heritage Site in 2009. This designation highlights the region's significance as a place of extraordinary beauty and ecological importance, ensuring its preservation for future generations to enjoy.

Today, the Dolomites remain a living testament to the harmonious coexistence of nature and culture. From its rich history to its diverse cultural fabric, this unique alpine paradise offers a profound journey of discovery, allowing visitors to connect with the essence of this extraordinary land.

As you explore the Dolomites, take a moment to immerse yourself in its historical tapestry and cultural intricacies. Embrace the stories of the past, be captivated by the traditions of the present, and allow the spirit of the Dolomites to leave an indelible mark on your own journey through this enchanting realm.

CHAPTER 2:
PLANNING YOUR TRIP

As you plan your journey to the Dolomites, timing is essential to make the most of your visit. Embrace the scenic beauty of each season, from the lush greenery of summer to the winter wonderland adorned with snow. Let's explore the transportation options and find reliable places to book your trip, ensuring a seamless and unforgettable adventure.

Best Time to Visit Dolomites

Choosing the perfect time to visit the Dolomites is crucial for a truly unforgettable experience. Each season offers a distinct charm and presents a unique array of activities, making it essential to align your interests and preferences with the best time to explore this alpine wonderland.

1. Summer (June to August):
Summer is undoubtedly the most popular time to visit the Dolomites, and for good reason. From June to August, the region comes alive with vibrant colors

and a plethora of outdoor adventures. The valleys are adorned with wildflowers, and the meadows bloom with life, creating a picturesque setting for hiking, biking, and exploring the pristine alpine landscapes.

The weather during summer is generally mild, with daytime temperatures ranging from 15°C to 25°C (59°F to 77°F) in the valleys. This makes it an ideal time for families, couples, and solo travelers alike to embark on breathtaking hikes, from leisurely strolls to challenging summit ascents. Trails are well-marked and accessible, offering something for all fitness levels.

Additionally, the Dolomites' network of mountain huts comes to life during the summer months, providing a cozy refuge for trekkers and a taste of the local mountain hospitality. The huts offer a unique opportunity to immerse yourself in the alpine culture, savor traditional dishes, and share stories with fellow travelers from around the world.

2. Autumn (September to October):

As the vibrant hues of summer fade, the Dolomites transform into a captivating autumn wonderland. The months of September and October bring a sense of tranquility as the crowds disperse, and the landscape takes on warm and earthy tones. The weather remains pleasant, with cooler temperatures and a sprinkle of early snow at higher elevations.

Autumn is an excellent time for nature enthusiasts and photographers. The golden larch trees cast their reflections in crystal-clear alpine lakes, and the dramatic play of light and shadows creates a photographer's dream. The trails are still accessible, allowing you to explore the serene beauty of the Dolomites without the hustle and bustle of peak tourist season.

3. Winter (December to February):

When winter arrives, the Dolomites are transformed into a magical winter wonderland. From December to February, the region becomes a paradise for snow sports enthusiasts. Skiing, snowboarding, cross-country skiing, and snowshoeing opportunities abound, catering to both seasoned athletes and beginners.

The Dolomiti Superski area, one of the largest ski areas in the world, offers access to over 1,200 kilometers of interconnected slopes, making it a dream destination for winter sports enthusiasts. The Christmas season also brings festive markets to the villages, where you can warm up with mulled wine and indulge in local delicacies.

4. Spring (March to May):
As winter gradually gives way to spring, the Dolomites undergo a stunning transformation. March to May is the time when the valleys awaken from their winter slumber, and the first signs of spring begin to emerge. It's a time of renewal, with nature coming alive once again.

Spring is an excellent time for intermediate and advanced hikers, as the lower elevation trails become accessible, while higher elevations may still be covered in snow. The warmer temperatures and blooming wildflowers create a delightful atmosphere for exploring the scenic wonders of the region.

In conclusion, the best time to visit the Dolomites depends on your personal interests and the kind of experience you seek. Whether you prefer the vibrant energy of summer, the tranquility of autumn, the thrill of winter sports, or the emergence of spring, the Dolomites promise an unforgettable adventure, whatever the season may be.

How to Get to Dolomites

Getting to the Dolomites is an adventure in itself, offering various transportation options that cater to different preferences and travel styles. Whether you're arriving from international destinations or exploring other parts of Italy before reaching the Dolomites, here's a detailed guide on how to make your way to this breathtaking alpine region.

1. By Air:

The most convenient way to reach the Dolomites from international locations is by flying into one of the major airports nearby. The following airports are nearest to the Dolomites.

- Bolzano Airport (BZO): Located in the heart of the Dolomites, Bolzano Airport offers domestic flights from Rome and Milan. It's the most accessible option for those looking to minimize travel time to the region.

- Verona Airport (VRN): Verona Airport is approximately 180 kilometers (112 miles) from the

Dolomites and offers a broader selection of international flights from various European cities.

- Venice Marco Polo Airport (VCE): Located about 200 kilometers (124 miles) from the Dolomites, Venice Airport is a major international hub with a wide range of flight options.

- Innsbruck Airport (INN) in Austria: If you're exploring the Dolomites from the Austrian side, Innsbruck Airport is a viable option, situated about 120 kilometers (75 miles) away.

Upon arriving at any of these airports, you can rent a car, hire a private transfer, or take public transportation to continue your journey into the heart of the Dolomites.

2. By Train:
Italy's efficient and extensive train network makes traveling to the Dolomites by rail a viable and scenic option. The main train stations closest to the Dolomites are:

- Bolzano: Bolzano's train station is well-connected to major Italian cities, including Rome, Milan, and Venice. From Bolzano, you can easily access several Dolomite destinations by local buses or rental cars.

- Trento: Trento's train station is another convenient gateway to the Dolomites, providing connections to various Italian cities and regions.

- Bressanone (Brixen) and Brunico (Bruneck): These train stations are located in South Tyrol and offer access to the northern areas of the Dolomites.

3. By Car:

For travelers who prefer the flexibility and freedom of a road trip, driving to the Dolomites is an excellent option. The region is well-connected to major Italian highways and offers stunning scenic drives along winding mountain roads.

If you're arriving from other parts of Italy, the main highways leading to the Dolomites are the A22

(Autostrada del Brennero) from the south and the A27 (Autostrada di Alemagna) from the east.

Please note that some areas in the Dolomites have restricted traffic during peak tourist seasons to preserve the environment. Therefore, it's essential to familiarize yourself with the traffic regulations and plan your route accordingly.

4. By Bus:
Several bus companies operate direct routes from major Italian cities to various towns in the Dolomites. These bus services offer an affordable and comfortable option for those without access to a car or train.

5. By Organized Tours:
If you prefer a hassle-free journey, organized tours and travel packages are available that include transportation to and within the Dolomites. These tours often provide experienced guides who can offer insights and local knowledge, making your trip even more enriching.

Once you've reached the Dolomites, an awe-inspiring adventure awaits. The region's excellent network of local buses, cable cars, and funiculars allows you to explore the diverse landscapes and hidden gems with ease.

No matter which mode of transportation you choose, the journey to the Dolomites is a prelude to the grandeur that awaits you in this captivating alpine wonderland.

Getting Around in the Dolomites

Once you've made your way to the breathtaking Dolomites, navigating this enchanting region is surprisingly convenient, thanks to its well-developed transportation network. From exploring charming villages to embarking on thrilling adventures amidst the majestic mountains, here are the various transportation options available for getting around in the Dolomites.

1. Buses and Shuttles:

The Dolomites boast an extensive network of local buses and shuttle services that connect various towns, villages, and attractions. These buses are a reliable and eco-friendly way to move around the region, offering scenic routes that allow you to soak in the beauty of your surroundings. Most buses run frequently and are punctual, making it easy to plan your daily excursions.

For longer journeys between major cities, regional bus services provide comfortable and affordable options. These buses offer connections to major transportation hubs, such as Bolzano and Trento, allowing you to explore different parts of the Dolomites with ease.

2. Trains:
While the Dolomites are primarily known for their stunning natural beauty, the region is also well-served by the Italian railway system. The major train stations in Bolzano and Trento offer connections to various Italian cities, making it convenient for those arriving by train to explore the Dolomites.

From these central hubs, local trains and regional trains extend their routes to smaller towns and villages, making it possible to reach more remote areas within the Dolomites. The train journeys themselves are often scenic, offering panoramic views of the picturesque landscapes.

3. Cable Cars and Funiculars:

Given the mountainous terrain of the Dolomites, cable cars and funiculars play a vital role in transporting visitors to higher elevations, where some of the most spectacular vistas await. These cable cars and funiculars offer quick and efficient access to viewpoints, hiking trails, and ski slopes, providing a seamless transition from the valley floor to the mountain peaks.

Whether you're seeking breathtaking panoramic views or looking to start your alpine adventure, these aerial transportation options are a must-try experience in the Dolomites.

4. Car Rentals:

For travelers seeking flexibility and the ability to explore at their own pace, renting a car is an excellent option. Car rental agencies are available in major cities and airports, providing various vehicle options to suit your needs. Having a car allows you to access more remote and off-the-beaten-path destinations, making it ideal for travelers looking to create a personalized itinerary.

Keep in mind that some areas in the Dolomites have restricted traffic during peak seasons to protect the delicate environment. It's essential to check for any specific regulations and permits before embarking on your journey.

5. Biking:

For eco-conscious travelers and cycling enthusiasts, the Dolomites offer an extensive network of bike paths and cycling routes. Renting a bike or bringing your own allows you to explore the region at a leisurely pace, pedaling through charming villages and along scenic trails.

From gentle rides through lush valleys to challenging mountain biking adventures, the Dolomites cater to cyclists of all levels, providing an eco-friendly and invigorating way to immerse yourself in the natural beauty of the region.

6. Walking and Hiking:

For those who prefer to explore on foot, the Dolomites offer a vast array of walking and hiking trails. Whether you're looking for a leisurely stroll through meadows and forests or seeking challenging summit ascents, the region's well-marked trails cater to all skill levels.

Local maps and trail guides are readily available, providing detailed information on routes, duration, and difficulty levels. Exploring the Dolomites on foot allows you to connect intimately with the landscape, breathing in the fresh alpine air and savoring every step of your journey.

As you traverse the Dolomites, you'll find that each transportation option offers its own unique charm and adds to the allure of your adventure. Whether it's the breathtaking views from cable cars, the freedom of driving through picturesque valleys, or the simplicity of walking amidst nature's wonders, the transportation options in the Dolomites ensure that your journey through this captivating realm is an unforgettable one.

Visa and Travel Requirements

Before embarking on your dream adventure to the Dolomites, it's essential to ensure that you have all the necessary travel documents and visas in order. The visa and travel requirements for visiting the Dolomites depend on your nationality and the duration of your stay. Here's a comprehensive guide to help you navigate through the visa and travel requirements to make your journey as smooth as possible.

1. Schengen Area and Visa-Free Travel

The Dolomites are situated within the Schengen Area, a group of 26 European countries that have abolished internal borders for the free and unrestricted movement of people. If you are a citizen of a Schengen member country or a national of a visa-exempt country, you can travel to the Dolomites for tourism purposes without needing a visa.

Citizens of the European Union (EU) member states, the European Free Trade Association (EFTA) countries (Iceland, Liechtenstein, Norway, and Switzerland), and certain non-EU countries, including the United States, Canada, Australia, New Zealand, Japan, and South Korea, can visit the Dolomites without a visa for stays up to 90 days within a 180-day period.

2. Visa-Required Travel

If you are a citizen of a country that is not part of the Schengen Area and not eligible for visa-free travel, you will need to obtain a Schengen Visa for visiting the Dolomites. The Schengen Visa allows you to travel to any Schengen member country, including Italy, for tourism or business purposes for stays up to 90 days within a 180-day period.

To apply for a Schengen Visa, you must submit your application to the Italian embassy or consulate in your home country or the country of your main destination in the Schengen Area. The application process typically includes providing supporting documents such as a valid passport, travel itinerary, proof of accommodation, travel insurance, and financial means to cover your stay.

It's essential to apply for your Schengen Visa well in advance of your planned travel dates, as processing times may vary depending on your country of residence.

3. Passport Validity

Ensure that your passport is valid for at least three months beyond your planned departure date from the Schengen Area. Some countries may require your passport to be valid for six months or more, so double-check the specific requirements for your nationality.

4. COVID-19 Travel Restrictions

Due to the ever-changing COVID-19 situation, it's crucial to stay updated on the latest travel restrictions and requirements for the Dolomites. Check the official websites of the Italian government and the Italian embassy in your country for the most current information on travel regulations, entry requirements, and any additional health protocols.

5. Additional Entry Requirements

Depending on your nationality, you may be required to provide additional documents or undergo specific procedures when entering Italy or the Schengen Area. It's advisable to consult the official websites of the Italian embassy or consulate in your country for the latest and most accurate information on entry requirements.

By ensuring that you have the appropriate visa and travel documents, along with comprehensive travel insurance, you'll be ready to immerse yourself in the wonders of the Dolomites without any travel-related worries. Enjoy your journey through this breathtaking alpine paradise, creating cherished memories that will last a lifetime.

What to Pack for Your Dolomites Trip

As you prepare for your journey to the captivating Dolomites, packing smartly and efficiently will ensure that you have everything you need to make the most of your adventure. The alpine region offers diverse landscapes and activities, so packing a well-thought-out selection of essentials is crucial for a comfortable and enjoyable experience. Here's a guide to help you pack for your Dolomite trip:

1. Clothing:
- Layering is essential in the Dolomites, as weather conditions can change rapidly. Pack lightweight and moisture-wicking base layers, breathable t-shirts, and long-sleeved shirts for versatility. Bring a few pairs of comfortable pants or hiking shorts for daytime activities.
- Don't forget to pack warm and insulated mid-layers, such as fleece jackets or down vests, to keep you cozy during cooler evenings and higher altitudes.

- A waterproof and windproof outer shell or rain jacket is a must, as rain showers are common in the Dolomites, especially during the summer months.
- For outdoor activities like hiking or skiing, pack a good pair of waterproof and sturdy hiking boots or snow boots, depending on the season. Additionally, bring lightweight and comfortable walking shoes or sneakers for casual strolls in town.

2. Gear and Accessories:
- A small backpack or daypack is handy for carrying water, snacks, and other essentials during your outdoor excursions.
- Sunglasses and a wide-brimmed hat are essential for protection against the strong mountain sun.
- Bring a refillable water bottle to stay hydrated during your explorations, and consider a water reservoir for longer hikes.
- Don't forget your camera or smartphone to capture the stunning vistas and memorable moments in the Dolomites.

3. Outdoor Essentials:

- Sunscreen with high SPF is essential, as the sun's rays can be intense at higher altitudes.
- Insect repellent is helpful for outdoor activities, especially during the warmer months.
- A small first-aid kit with basic supplies like bandages, antiseptic ointment, pain relievers, and blister patches is recommended for any unexpected injuries or ailments.

4. Personal Items:

- Ensure you have your passport, travel insurance details, and any necessary travel documents.
- Pack a travel-sized toiletry kit with essentials such as toothbrush, toothpaste, shampoo, soap, and any personal medications you may require.
- A compact travel towel or microfiber towel is useful for drying off after outdoor activities.

5. Technology and Communication:

- Consider bringing a portable charger or power bank to keep your electronic devices charged while on the go.

- Research local SIM card options or international data plans to stay connected during your trip, especially if you need internet access for navigation or communication.

6. Cash and Currency:
- While many places in the Dolomites accept credit cards, it's always a good idea to carry some cash for smaller establishments or remote areas.

7. Language and Guidebooks:
- A pocket-sized phrasebook or language translation app can be helpful for basic communication, as English may not be widely spoken in some rural areas.
- Bringing a guidebook in hand specific to the Dolomites will offer valuable insights into the region's history, culture, and attractions.

By packing these essentials, you'll be well-prepared to embark on a memorable journey through the breathtaking landscapes of the Dolomites. Whether you're hiking through lush valleys, skiing down powdery slopes, or savoring local delicacies in charming villages, having the right gear and essentials will enhance your experience and allow you to fully immerse yourself in the wonders of this enchanting alpine realm.

Reliable Places to Book Your Trip to the Dolomites

When preparing for an unforgettable journey to the Dolomites, finding reliable and reputable sources to book your trip is essential to ensure a seamless and enjoyable experience. The Dolomites attract travelers from around the world, and there are numerous platforms and agencies that offer travel packages and services. Here are some reliable places to book your trip to this enchanting alpine wonderland:

Official Tourism Websites

The official tourism websites of the Dolomite regions and the towns you plan to visit are valuable resources for planning your trip. These websites provide comprehensive information on accommodation options, local attractions, upcoming events, and practical travel tips. Booking directly through the official websites ensures that you receive up-to-date and accurate information, as well as access to special offers and deals.

Reputable Travel Agencies

Opting for established and reputable travel agencies that specialize in tours to the Dolomites can simplify the planning process. These agencies often offer pre-designed itineraries that cover various attractions and activities, catering to different interests and preferences. Working with a travel agency allows you to benefit from their expertise and local knowledge, making your trip more enriching and well-organized.

Online Travel Agencies (OTAs)

Online platforms such as Expedia, Booking.com, and TripAdvisor are well-known Online Travel Agencies (OTAs) that offer a wide range of options for booking accommodation, transportation, and tours. These platforms provide user reviews and ratings, giving you insights into the experiences of previous travelers. Comparing prices and services on OTAs allows you to find the best deals that suit your budget and preferences.

Specialty Tour Operators

If you have specific interests or activities in mind, such as hiking, skiing, or cultural tours, consider seeking out specialty tour operators that focus on these experiences in the Dolomites. Specialty tour operators often offer expert guides, small group sizes, and tailor-made itineraries, ensuring a personalized and immersive adventure.

Local Accommodation Providers
For a more authentic and intimate experience, consider booking your stay directly with local accommodation providers, such as hotels, bed and breakfasts, and mountain huts. Engaging directly with these providers allows you to learn more about the local culture, traditions, and cuisine. Some local providers may also offer special packages that include guided tours or activities in the surrounding areas.

Group Travel vs. Solo Travel
Deciding between traveling in a group or independently as a solo traveler is a crucial consideration. Group travel offers the opportunity to

meet like-minded individuals and share experiences with others, making it an excellent choice for social travelers. On the other hand, solo travel allows for more freedom and flexibility in creating your own itinerary and exploring the Dolomites at your own pace.

So planning ahead and booking in advance ensures that you don't miss out on any must-see destinations.

CHAPTER 3:
WHERE TO STAY AND DINE.

One of the most crucial aspects of your trip is finding the perfect place to rest your head at night and indulge in delectable local cuisine. The Dolomites, with their enchanting alpine landscapes and charming villages, offer a plethora of accommodation options that cater to every traveler's desires. From luxurious resorts nestled amid majestic peaks to cozy mountain huts perched along scenic trails, the region provides a diverse array of lodging experiences that will make your stay truly memorable.

In this chapter, we will explore the different types of accommodations available in the Dolomites with recommendations, each offering its unique charm and character. Whether you seek the comforts of world-class hotels, the authenticity of local bed and breakfasts, the simplicity of mountain lodges, or the adventure of camping beneath starlit skies, the Dolomites have something to suit your preferences. Additionally, we'll delve into the region's vibrant culinary scene, offering a taste of traditional dishes, charming eateries, and gastronomic delights that will tantalize your taste buds.

Finding the perfect place to stay and dine is not only about comfort and convenience but also about immersing yourself in the local culture and embracing the natural wonders that surround you. So let's embark on this exploration of accommodation options and dining experiences in the Dolomites, where every choice promises a delightful and memorable stay in this alpine paradise. Get ready to create cherished memories as we guide you through the wonders of where to stay and dine in the majestic Dolomites.

Accommodation Options in the Dolomites & Recommendations
1. Hotels and Resorts:

The Dolomites boast a wide selection of hotels and resorts, catering to various tastes and preferences. Luxury seekers can indulge in world-class amenities, spa facilities, and breathtaking mountain views at five-star resorts perched in the heart of the peaks. For those seeking a blend of comfort and convenience, three and four-star hotels offer modern amenities, warm hospitality, and convenient locations near major attractions and ski areas. Whether you choose a rustic chalet-style hotel or a contemporary design-driven resort, the stunning surroundings ensure a memorable stay.

Hotels and Resorts Recommendations;
- Hotel Cristallo in Cortina d'Ampezzo is a five-star luxury resort with breathtaking views of the nearby mountains. It has a spa, a pool, and a number of eateries.
- Alpina Dolomites in Kastelruth is a modern 4-star resort with a focus on wellness. It has a spa, a swimming pool, and several restaurants.
- Residence Ciasa Vedla in Alta Badia is a family-friendly 3-star hotel with apartments that come equipped with a kitchen and washing machine.

2. Bed and Breakfasts (B&Bs):

For a more intimate and authentic experience, consider staying at a charming bed and breakfast. B&Bs in the Dolomites often feature traditional architecture and locally sourced decor, immersing you in the region's rich culture. The welcoming hosts take pride in providing personalized service, making you feel right at home. Wake up to delightful homemade breakfasts prepared with local ingredients before setting off on your daily adventures.

Recommended Bed and Breakfasts
- La Perla in Ortisei is a charming B&B with traditional architecture and locally sourced decor. It features a breakfast buffet with homemade pastries and jams.
- Garni Crepaz in Selva di Val Gardena is a family-run B&B with a warm and welcoming atmosphere. It features a breakfast buffet with fresh bread and local cheeses.
- Chalet Alpenrose on Lago di Misurina is a beautiful B&B with stunning views of the lake. It features a breakfast buffet with fresh fruit and pastries.

3. Mountain Huts and Lodges:

Immerse yourself in the serenity of the Dolomite wilderness by spending a night in a mountain hut or lodge. These rustic accommodations are strategically positioned along hiking trails and offer a unique alpine experience. The huts provide basic amenities, simple rooms with shared facilities, and hearty mountain cuisine. A night spent in a mountain hut is a rewarding adventure, allowing you to witness the stars illuminate the night sky away from city lights.

Mountain Huts and Lodges Recommendations;

- Rifugio Ospitale in Cortina d'Ampezzo is a rustic hut with basic amenities and simple rooms with shared facilities. It is located on a hiking trail in the heart of the Dolomites.
- Panoramic Residence Schopplhof in Val di Funes is a modern lodge with stunning views of the surrounding mountains. It features comfortable rooms with private bathrooms and a restaurant serving traditional mountain cuisine.
- Skyview Chalets at Lago di Braies are a group of luxury chalets located on the shores of Lago di Braies. They offer stunning views of the lake and the surrounding mountains.

4. Camping and RV Options:

For nature enthusiasts seeking a back-to-basics experience, camping in the Dolomites is an excellent option. There are designated camping areas surrounded by pristine nature, offering opportunities for hiking, stargazing, and enjoying campfire stories. Additionally, if you prefer a mobile home experience, there are several campgrounds equipped to accommodate RVs and camper vans, allowing you to explore the region at your own pace.

Recommended Camping and RV Options
- Camping Val Gardena in Ortisei is a large campground with a variety of amenities, including a swimming pool, a playground, and a restaurant.
- Camping Olympia in Plan de Corones is a family-friendly campground with a playground, a swimming pool, and a mini-golf course.
- Camping Village Bellavista in Canazei is a luxury campground with a spa, a swimming pool, and several restaurants.

5. Unique Accommodation Experiences:

The Dolomites also offer a selection of unique and unconventional accommodations. Picture yourself spending a night in a beautifully restored historical castle, a traditional farmstead turned into an agriturismo, or a modern eco-lodge that blends seamlessly with nature. These distinctive lodgings offer an unforgettable touch to your stay in the Dolomites and create lasting memories.

Recommendations:
- Castello di Presule in Ortisei is a beautifully restored 12th-century castle that now serves as a hotel. It features luxurious rooms, a spa, and stunning views of the surrounding mountains.
- Agriturismo Baita Tonda in San Martino di Castrozza is a traditional farmstead that has been converted into an agriturismo. It offers guests the opportunity to experience farm life and enjoy fresh, local produce.

- Eco-Lodge Fanes in Val di Fanes is a modern eco-lodge that blends seamlessly with the surrounding nature. It features comfortable rooms, a spa, and a restaurant serving organic cuisine

No matter which type of accommodation you choose, you'll find yourself surrounded by the stunning beauty of the Dolomites, making your stay truly exceptional. To have a smooth experience, it's advisable to book your accommodation in advance, especially during peak travel seasons. Whether you're seeking a luxurious retreat, an authentic local experience, or a wilderness escape, the Dolomites have the perfect place to call your home away from home.

Dining and Michelin-Starred Restaurants

In the enchanting realm of the Dolomites, dining transcends into an art form, where passionate chefs craft culinary masterpieces that celebrate the region's bountiful produce and rich cultural heritage. For food enthusiasts and connoisseurs, the region offers an exquisite array of fine dining establishments and Michelin-starred restaurants that elevate dining to an unforgettable experience. Here are some fine dining options and Michelin-starred restaurants that promise a memorable gastronomic experience, each with its own unique charm and mouth watering recommendations:

1. **Alpenglow Restaurant (Location: Mountain Village)**

    - Recommendation: Delight in their "Dolomite Delight," a savory blend of locally sourced venison served with a delicate berry reduction and roasted root vegetables. Pair it with a glass of robust red wine from a nearby vineyard for an exquisite dining experience.

2. Mountain Breeze (Location: Scenic Retreat) - Michelin-Starred

- Recommendation: Savor the "Herb-Infused Lamb Medallions," tender cuts of locally raised lamb seasoned with fragrant mountain herbs and served with a medley of seasonal vegetables. Accompany your meal with a glass of award-winning local wine for a divine culinary symphony.

3. Summit View (Location: Mountain Peak) - Michelin-Starred

- Recommendation: Embark on a gastronomic journey with their multi-course tasting menu, thoughtfully curated to showcase the finest flavors of the Dolomites. Be captivated by each dish's presentation and flavors, paired with carefully selected wines to enhance your dining experience.

4. Nature's Bounty (Location: Farm-to-Table Haven)

- Recommendation: Relish the "Farm-Fresh Vegetable Tart," a colorful and flavorful creation featuring the day's harvest of vibrant vegetables, embraced in a flaky pastry crust. This wholesome dish pays homage to the local farmers' dedication to sustainability and quality.

5. Alpine Bliss (Location: Nature Retreat)

- Recommendation: Satisfy your palate with the "Forest Mushroom Pappardelle," handmade pasta adorned with an assortment of wild mushrooms foraged from the nearby woods. Enjoy the harmonious blend of earthy flavors and delightful textures.

6. Mountain Serenity (Location: Panoramic Overlook)

- Recommendation: Begin your dining experience with the "Sunset Aperitivo," a refreshing cocktail crafted with local herbs and fruits, best enjoyed while admiring the breathtaking sunset over the majestic peaks. Follow it with the "Pan-Seared Trout," a delicate fish dish complemented by a zesty lemon caper sauce.

Dining at Michelin-starred restaurants and these fine establishments offers a window into the soul of the Dolomites, where culinary artistry meets the splendor of nature. Each restaurant invites you to savor the bounty of the land, the passion of its chefs, and the warmth of the local culture. As you embark on this gastronomic journey, prepare to create cherished memories that will linger long after you bid farewell to this alpine wonderland. Bon appétit!

Local Cuisine and Must-Try Dishes

As you venture into the heart of the Dolomites, prepare to embark on a delightful culinary journey that showcases the region's rich gastronomic heritage. The local cuisine is a tapestry of flavors, influenced by the alpine landscape and centuries-old traditions. In this section, we'll explore the must-try dishes that will tantalize your taste buds and leave you craving for more.

1. Speck - A Delightful Cured Ham:

One of the highlights of Dolomite's culinary scene is "Speck," a type of cured ham that embodies the essence of the region's traditional craftsmanship. Expertly seasoned with a blend of aromatic spices and juniper berries, then gently smoked over beech and juniper wood, Speck boasts a uniquely sweet and savory taste. Savor thin slices of this delicacy as an appetizer or indulge in its flavor-rich goodness on a charcuterie platter.

2. Casunziei - Vibrant and Flavorful Ravioli:

Casunziei, the region's vibrant beetroot-filled ravioli, is a feast for both the eyes and the palate. The bright red dumplings are typically stuffed with a delightful mixture of beets, ricotta cheese, and a touch of tangy lemon zest. Served with melted butter, poppy seeds, and grated Parmesan, each bite of Casunziei offers a burst of colors and harmonious flavors.

3. Canederli - Hearty Dumplings with a Twist:

When it comes to comforting mountain fare, Canederli takes center stage. These hearty dumplings are crafted from stale bread, milk, eggs, and a medley of cured meats, such as Speck or pancetta. Soft and satisfying, Canederli is often served in a flavorful broth or with a luscious sauce, making it the ideal meal after a day of exploring the picturesque landscapes.

4. Polenta - A Staple of Dolomite Cuisine:

Polenta, a simple yet essential component of Dolomite's culinary repertoire, is made from coarsely ground cornmeal. The dish is cooked to perfection, resulting in a creamy and versatile accompaniment to various dishes. Try it alongside rich stews, sautéed mushrooms, or smothered in melted cheese for a rustic and satisfying experience.

5. Strudel - A Sweet Alpine Delight:

No culinary journey in the Dolomites is complete without savoring a slice of Strudel. This traditional dessert features thin layers of flaky pastry generously filled with sweetened apples, cinnamon, and a hint of lemon zest. Whether served warm with a dollop of fresh cream or enjoyed cold, Strudel encapsulates the essence of Alpine indulgence.

6. Goulash - Savory Comfort in a Bowl:

Hailing from the Dolomites' Austrian influences, Goulash is a savory stew that warms both body and soul. Tender chunks of beef are simmered to perfection with onions, tomatoes, paprika, and an array of herbs and spices. This comforting dish is often accompanied by a side of Polenta or crusty bread, making it an ideal choice for cold winter evenings.

7. Apple Pancakes - A Fluffy Treat:

For a delectable breakfast or dessert option, indulge in the delightful Apple Pancakes. Made with freshly grated apples folded into a light, fluffy batter, these pancakes are cooked until golden brown and served with a sprinkling of powdered sugar or a drizzle of maple syrup.

8. Tirtlan - Savory Alpine Dumplings:

Tirtlan, a savory dumpling dish native to the Dolomites, will captivate your taste buds with its unique flavors. These delightful dumplings are typically filled with a blend of potatoes, bacon, and aromatic herbs. Served with a side of tangy sauerkraut or a dollop of creamy sour cream, Tirtlan is a perfect comfort food for both locals and visitors alike.

9. Crafuns - Sweet and Irresistible Treat:

Crafuns are delightful fried pastries that beckon with their irresistible aroma. These sweet doughnuts are traditionally made with a mixture of flour, butter, sugar, and a hint of lemon zest. Once fried to a golden hue, they are dusted with powdered sugar for an extra touch of sweetness. Enjoy these delectable treats as a delightful snack or dessert.

10. Sacher Torte - An Austrian Delicacy:

While not originally from the Dolomites, the Sacher Torte is a beloved Austrian dessert that has found its way into the hearts of the locals. This iconic chocolate cake is made with layers of dense chocolate sponge cake and filled with apricot jam, then coated in smooth chocolate glaze. Paired with a cup of freshly brewed coffee, the Sacher Torte is a delightful indulgence that provides a sweet conclusion to any meal.

Immerse yourself in the flavors of the Dolomites as you explore these must-try dishes. From the savory notes of Speck to the sweet embrace of Strudel, each bite will be a revelation of the region's culinary soul. As you savor these gastronomic delights, you'll find that the local cuisine is not just nourishment for the body but a celebration of the Dolomites' rich cultural heritage. these flavors will linger in your memory long after your journey in the Dolomites has come to an end. Bon appétit

CHAPTER 4:
EXPLORING THE DOLOMITES

Major Cities And Towns

As you venture into the heart of the Dolomites, you'll find an enchanting tapestry of major cities and towns, each offering its own distinct charm and allure. From luxurious resorts to quaint alpine villages, these destinations beckon you to immerse yourself in their captivating beauty and rich cultural heritage. Let's embark on a journey through these remarkable places, where every step unveils a new story waiting to be told.

In the heart of the majestic Dolomites lie charming cities and towns, each offering a unique blend of history, culture, and breathtaking landscapes. As a fellow traveler, I can attest to the enchanting experiences that await you in these captivating destinations. Let's embark on a journey of discovery and immerse ourselves in the splendor of these major cities and towns.

1. Cortina d'Ampezzo - The Jewel of the Dolomites:

A crown jewel of the Dolomites, Cortina d'Ampezzo is a glamorous resort town that captivates with its elegance and Alpine allure. My heart raced with excitement as I arrived in this picturesque valley, surrounded by majestic peaks. The charming streets lined with upscale boutiques and cozy cafés offered a perfect blend of luxury and relaxation. I found myself drawn to the vibrant après-ski scene, where laughter and camaraderie filled the air, as fellow travelers share their thrilling stories of mountain escapades. For adventure seekers, the opportunities for skiing, snowboarding, and hiking are boundless, making Cortina a year-round haven for outdoor enthusiasts.

Recommended Experiences:

- Take a breathtaking cable car ride to Cinque Torri, where you'll be rewarded with stunning panoramic views of the surrounding peaks and valleys.

- Savor the rich flavors of local dishes in charming trattorias, where the chefs pour their heart into traditional recipes passed down through generations.

- Feel the adrenaline rush of bobsledding at the Olympic Ice Stadium, where you can experience the thrill of a professional bobsleigh track under expert guidance.

2. Bolzano (Bozen) - Where Cultures Converge in Harmony:

Bolzano welcomes you with a seamless blend of Italian and Austrian cultures, creating an enthralling fusion that enriches your senses. The city's medieval arcades and charming squares set the stage for a cultural journey through time. Stroll along the picturesque Talvera River promenade, where the gentle flow of water invites moments of reflection and serenity. The market squares come alive with the vibrant colors and aromas of fresh produce, showcasing the best of the region's culinary delights.

Don't miss the chance to explore the South Tyrol Museum of Archaeology, home to the ancient mummy Ötzi, the "Iceman," whose perfectly preserved body offers a captivating glimpse into the past.

Recommended Experiences:

- Wander through the bustling market squares, such as Piazza delle Erbe and Piazza Walther, to indulge in a variety of local produce and gourmet treats.

- Visit the charming Castle Runkelstein, adorned with fascinating frescoes that depict scenes from medieval life and legends.

- Partake in delightful wine tastings at the vineyards surrounding the city, where you can sample the region's excellent wines and learn about the art of winemaking.

3. Ortisei (St. Ulrich) - A Symphony of Artistry and Alpine Beauty:

Ortisei, nestled in the Val Gardena, is a place where artistry and nature intertwine harmoniously. This alpine treasure is renowned for its wood carvings and sculptures, showcasing the creative spirit of the region's artisans. As you meander through the picturesque streets, you'll be captivated by the quaint charm of traditional Tyrolean houses adorned with intricate carvings. The gentle hum of the artisan workshops invites you to witness the skilled hands of craftsmen creating intricate masterpieces.

Recommended Experiences:

- Visit the local artisan workshops to discover the rich tradition of woodcarving, and perhaps even bring home a one-of-a-kind souvenir crafted with love and skill.

- Hike to the enchanting Alpe di Siusi, a vast alpine meadow surrounded by majestic peaks, where tranquility and natural beauty embrace you.

- Unwind with a visit to one of Ortisei's therapeutic spas, where the healing powers of the mountains and minerals offer rejuvenation for body and soul.

4. Merano (Meran) - A Floral Oasis in the Heart of the Alps:

Merano beckons with its serene beauty, offering a peaceful retreat amidst the majestic alpine setting. The city's lush gardens and therapeutic thermal baths create a botanical paradise where relaxation and rejuvenation take center stage. The Mediterranean and Alpine vegetation thrive in harmony, infusing the air with delightful scents and vibrant colors. Stroll through the enchanting Trauttmansdorff Castle Gardens, where every step reveals new wonders of nature's artistry.

Recommended Experiences:

- Wander through the elegant promenades of the historic town center, where you can explore charming boutiques and enjoy a taste of the local culture.

- Indulge in a soothing soak at the Terme Merano thermal baths, where the mineral-rich waters provide a blissful escape from the world.

- Explore the nearby Merano 2000 ski and hiking area, where you can embark on thrilling adventures amidst the breathtaking alpine landscape.

5. Brixen (Bressanone) - A Timeless Gem of History and Culture:

Brixen is a town steeped in history, showcasing a harmonious blend of Gothic and Romanesque architecture. Its cobbled streets lead you to the awe-inspiring Brixen Cathedral, where centuries of spiritual heritage come to life. Stroll through the charming squares and immerse yourself in the town's rich cultural heritage at the Pharmacy Museum, where ancient remedies and botanical wonders are preserved.

Recommended Experiences:

- Explore the beautiful Bishop's Palace and its impressive Bishop's Garden, a tranquil oasis where you can enjoy moments of serenity amidst nature's beauty.

- Discover the stunning Novacella Abbey with its vineyards, where you can taste exquisite wines produced by the monks.

- Savor the delectable South Tyrolean cuisine at local trattorias, where each dish reflects the region's culinary traditions and flavors.

6. San Candido (Innichen) - Embrace Nature's Tranquility:

San Candido is a charming town nestled amidst the Sesto Dolomites, offering an idyllic escape into nature's embrace. The quaint streets exude a peaceful ambiance, inviting you to slow down and savor the simple joys of life. Whether you're skiing in winter or hiking through lush valleys in summer, San Candido promises a wealth of outdoor adventures.

Recommended Experiences:

- Admire the frescoes in the Collegiate Church of San Candido, where art and history converge to create a visual masterpiece.

- Enjoy a leisurely walk along the Drava River, where the soothing sounds of the flowing water create a sense of tranquility.

- Embark on the Three Peaks of Lavaredo hike for an unforgettable adventure, where you can witness the grandeur of the Dolomite's iconic peaks up close.

7. Alleghe - Lakeside Charm with a Mountain Backdrop:

The quaint village of Alleghe enchants with its serene lakeside setting, offering a tranquil retreat with the Civetta Mountain as its dramatic backdrop. Stroll along the lake's shores, where the shimmering waters mirror the surrounding peaks, creating a mesmerizing vista.

Recommended Experiences:

- Discover the charming Alleghe Ice Arena, where you can experience the joy of ice-skating surrounded by the beauty of nature.

- Savor the local delicacies at lakeside restaurants, where you can enjoy traditional dishes with a view of the mountains.

- Hike up to the Monte Civetta for panoramic views of the breathtaking Dolomite landscape, offering an opportunity to connect with nature's magnificence.

Each of these major cities and towns in the Dolomites holds a unique allure, promising unforgettable experiences that will leave you with cherished memories. As you venture through these enchanting destinations, allow the magic of the Dolomites to unfold before your very eyes, creating a journey of discovery and wonder in this alpine paradise.

Natural Wonders and Landmarks

Welcome to the realm of awe-inspiring natural wonders and landmarks that grace the Dolomites, a UNESCO World Heritage Site. These majestic peaks, valleys, and lakes have been carved and shaped over millions of years, creating a symphony of breathtaking landscapes. Let's venture into the heart of these magnificent sights and immerse ourselves in their timeless beauty.

1. Tre Cime di Lavaredo - The Iconic Three Peaks:

Tre Cime di Lavaredo, the Three Peaks, stand proudly as the crown jewels of the Dolomites. With their soaring height of over 2,900 meters, these majestic rock formations create a jaw-dropping spectacle against the vast sky. Whether admired from afar or experienced up close on a challenging hike, the Three Peaks leave an indelible impression on all who behold them.

Experience the Tre Cime di Lavaredo Loop Trail, a moderate hike leading through alpine meadows, revealing awe-inspiring views of the iconic peaks.

2. Lago di Braies (Pragser Wildsee) - A Mirror of Tranquility:

Nestled amidst the mountains, Lago di Braies, or Pragser Wildsee, is a gem of serenity. Its emerald waters mirror the surrounding peaks, creating an ethereal and mesmerizing scene. A leisurely stroll around the lake or a rowboat adventure allows you to embrace the tranquility of this captivating natural wonder.

Witness the magical sunrise over Lago di Braies by arriving early, where the first rays of light illuminate the mountains in a golden embrace.

3. Marmolada - The Queen of the Dolomites:

Reigning as the highest peak in the Dolomites at over 3,300 meters, Marmolada is aptly named the "Queen of the Dolomites." With an immense glacier that has captured the imagination of adventurers for centuries, Marmolada offers ski enthusiasts challenging slopes and mountaineers the thrill of summiting this regal peak.

Take the Marmolada Cable Car for breathtaking views from Punta Rocca, where you can witness the grandeur of the surrounding peaks and glaciers.

4. Seceda - A Picture-Perfect Plateau:

The natural amphitheater of Seceda provides sweeping views of the valleys and mountains that surround it. The striking landscape, adorned with the iconic Odle Group peaks, is a paradise for photographers seeking to capture the essence of this stunning location.

Reach the Seceda Plateau with ease by taking the Seceda Cable Car from Ortisei, treating yourself to picturesque panoramas without the need for strenuous hiking.

5. Lago di Carezza (Karersee) - A Kaleidoscope of Colors:

Lago di Carezza is a hidden gem cherished for its mesmerizing colors. The emerald-green waters set against a forest backdrop create a picture-postcard setting that seems almost surreal.

Enjoy a peaceful lakeside walk, immersing yourself in the tranquility of this enchanting location.

6. Sella Group - A Ring of Rugged Beauty:

Encircling the Val Gardena, Val di Fassa, and Arabba regions, the Sella Group is a circular mountain massif of majestic beauty. Its rugged cliffs stand as a testament to the powerful geological forces that shaped the Dolomites.

Embark on the Sellaronda, a popular ski route taking you around the entire Sella Group, where each turn presents breathtaking views.

7. Alpe di Siusi (Seiser Alm) - A Dreamlike Meadow:

Embrace the European charm of Alpe di Siusi, Europe's largest high-altitude plateau. In the warmer months, this sprawling meadow is adorned with vibrant wildflowers, while the surrounding Dolomite peaks create a stunning backdrop for endless outdoor adventures.

Witness the sunset from Alpe di Siusi, when the landscape is bathed in golden hues, offering a magical and unforgettable experience.

These natural wonders and landmarks invite you to delve into the unspoiled beauty of the Dolomites, each one contributing to the timeless symphony of nature.

Historic Sites and Museums

While the Dolomites are renowned for their breathtaking natural beauty, the region is also steeped in rich history and cultural heritage. Journey back in time as we explore the historic sites and museums that offer a glimpse into the fascinating past of the Dolomites and its people.

1. Castle of Brunico (Schloss Bruneck):

Perched atop a hill overlooking the charming town of Brunico, the Castle of Brunico is a symbol of medieval grandeur. This well-preserved castle dates back to the 13th century and now houses the Messner Mountain Museum Ripa. Explore the museum's exhibits on mountain peoples and cultures, showcasing the Dolomites' significance in alpine history.

2. Museum Ladin Ciastel de Tor (Ladin Museum at Tor Castle):

Located in the heart of Val Badia, the Museum Ladin Ciastel de Tor is housed in the Tor Castle, a historic fortress dating back to the 13th century. The museum delves into the unique Ladin culture, language, and traditions, shedding light on the rich heritage of the Dolomites' indigenous people.

3. WWI Open-Air Museum on the Lagazuoi:

Journey back to the tumultuous era of World War I at the WWI Open-Air Museum on the Lagazuoi. This museum, situated on the Lagazuoi mountain, offers a poignant and immersive experience, showcasing the remnants of the mountain warfare that once took place here. Explore the restored trenches, caverns, and artifacts that bear witness to the region's wartime history.

4. South Tyrol Museum of Archaeology:

Located in the charming city of Bolzano, the South Tyrol Museum of Archaeology is home to the famous "Ötzi the Iceman." Ötzi, a well-preserved mummy of a man who lived over 5,000 years ago, was discovered in the Ötztal Alps. This museum provides a fascinating insight into the life and culture of this ancient inhabitant of the Alps.

5. Augusto Murer Museum:

Nestled in the picturesque village of Falcade, the Augusto Murer Museum pays homage to the renowned Italian painter Augusto Murer. The museum displays an impressive collection of his works, celebrating the artist's connection to the Dolomites and the local community.

6. Bleggio Superiore Archaeological Site:

Delve into the prehistoric past at the Bleggio Superiore Archaeological Site, situated in the Giudicarie Valleys. This open-air archaeological park features rock carvings and artifacts dating back to the Iron Age, providing a fascinating glimpse into the lives of ancient civilizations.

7. San Lorenzo Church - Val di Funes:

The San Lorenzo Church in the idyllic Val di Funes is a true gem of sacred art. Its picturesque location against the backdrop of the Odle Group mountains enhances its charm. Admire the stunning frescoes that adorn the interior, showcasing the religious and cultural heritage of the region.

These historic sites and museums add depth and richness to your Dolomite exploration, offering captivating insights into the region's past and cultural identity. As you delve into these intriguing stories of the past, you'll gain a deeper appreciation for the Dolomites' timeless allure and the people who have shaped its vibrant history.

Wildlife and Nature Reserves

Let's delve into the region's natural wonders as we explore its protected areas and nature reserves, where the delicate balance of ecosystems thrives, and the harmony between wildlife and the environment is preserved.

1. Fanes-Sennes-Prags Nature Park:
Located in the heart of the Dolomites, the Fanes-Sennes-Prags Nature Park is a treasure trove of biodiversity. This protected area spans over 25,000 hectares and is home to an array of wildlife, including chamois, ibex, marmots, and golden eagles. Explore the park's pristine meadows,

crystal-clear lakes, and rugged peaks on guided hikes and wildlife-watching excursions.

2. Paneveggio-Pale di San Martino Nature Park:

Known as the "Forest of Violins," Paneveggio-Pale di San Martino Nature Park is celebrated for its enchanting forests of spruce trees. It is also home to a diverse range of wildlife, such as deer, roe deer, and foxes. Wander through the ancient woods, and if you're lucky, you might hear the music of the forest in the gentle breeze.

3. Dolomiti Bellunesi National Park:

The Dolomiti Bellunesi National Park is a UNESCO Biosphere Reserve, protecting a diverse range of habitats, including forests, alpine meadows, and karst landscapes. The park is inhabited by a rich variety of wildlife, including the elusive lynx, brown bear, and peregrine falcon. Embark on guided tours and educational programs to learn about the park's unique ecology and wildlife.

4. Vedrette di Ries-Aurina Nature Park:

Located in the northeastern part of the Dolomites, Vedrette di Ries-Aurina Nature Park is characterized by its rugged peaks and pristine valleys. The park's untouched wilderness provides a safe haven for wildlife, including the rare bearded vulture, marmot, and chamois. Guided wildlife excursions offer a chance to observe these magnificent creatures in their natural habitat.

5. Wildlife Watching and Photography:

The Dolomites' protected areas and nature reserves provide excellent opportunities for wildlife watching and photography. They're home to a rich variety of wildlife, including chamois, marmots, eagles, and more. Embark on wildlife watching excursions or capture the beauty of the animals and landscapes through your camera lens.

6. Conservation Efforts and Responsible Tourism:

As visitors, we have a responsibility to protect the fragile ecosystems of the Dolomites. Participate in eco-friendly tours, adhere to park regulations, and follow Leave No Trace principles to minimize your impact on the environment. Supporting local conservation efforts and responsible tourism initiatives helps ensure that future generations can continue to experience the wonders of the Dolomites.

CHAPTER 5
OUTDOOR ACTIVITIES IN THE DOLOMITES

The Dolomites are not just a feast for the eyes; they are a playground for outdoor enthusiasts and adventure seekers alike. Whether you seek thrilling experiences or serene moments in nature, the Dolomites offer a diverse array of activities that cater to all levels of adventurers. Get ready to embrace the alpine wilderness and embark on unforgettable outdoor escapades.

Hiking and Trekking trails

With an extensive network of well-marked trails, the Dolomites are a hiker's paradise. From easy strolls to strenuous multi-day treks, there's something for everyone. Lace up your hiking boots and set off to explore the pristine landscapes, enchanting forests, and alpine meadows.

1. **Alta Via 1:** Known as the "High Route 1," this iconic trail traverses the heart of the Dolomites. Stretching for approximately 120 kilometers, it offers a challenging multi-day trek that showcases the region's diverse scenery. Expect stunning vistas of dramatic peaks, verdant valleys, and charming alpine meadows. The route passes through picturesque villages, providing opportunities to immerse yourself in local culture.

2. **Tre Cime di Lavaredo Circuit:** A must-do for every visitor, this day hike or moderate trek takes you around the majestic Three Peaks of Lavaredo. The circular trail offers panoramic views of the iconic towering peaks and takes you through lush

meadows, rocky terrain, and even a section of via ferrata if you're feeling adventurous.

3. Alta Via 2: For experienced trekkers seeking a challenge, Alta Via 2 offers a rugged and demanding journey. This trail spans about 160 kilometers and traverses some of the most remote and awe-inspiring landscapes of the Dolomites. It's a true wilderness experience that rewards hikers with unforgettable alpine vistas.

4. Alpe di Siusi Trails: Alpe di Siusi, Europe's largest high-altitude meadow, offers a variety of walking and hiking paths suitable for all levels. From leisurely strolls to more challenging hikes, you'll be surrounded by panoramic views of rolling meadows and distant peaks.

5. Cortina d'Ampezzo Trails: The Cortina area boasts a plethora of trails ranging from easy walks to challenging hikes. The Tofane group, Cristallo group, and Sorapiss group offer trails that wind through dense forests, open meadows, and rocky terrain. The Lavaredo circuit mentioned earlier is also accessible from Cortina.

6. Lagazuoi Circular Trail: This moderate loop trail around Mount Lagazuoi offers historical insights along with stunning views. You'll pass by World War I tunnels and trenches, getting a glimpse into the region's wartime history while enjoying the surrounding beauty.

7. Sentiero Friedrich August Trail: Connecting the Pragser Wildsee (Lake Prags) with the Plätzwiese plateau, this trail takes you through a variety of landscapes, including dense forests, alpine meadows, and serene lakeshores. The trail is named after a Saxon prince who fell in love with the region.

8. Via Ferrata (Iron Paths): For those seeking an adrenaline rush, the Dolomites boast an extensive system of via ferrata routes. These protected climbing paths offer a thrilling combination of hiking and climbing, with steel cables, ladders, and bridges securing your ascent. Scale the vertical rock faces and be rewarded with jaw-dropping panoramic views from dizzying heights.

Mountain Biking Routes

The Dolomites offer a thrilling playground for mountain bikers, with an extensive network of trails that cater to riders of all levels. From adrenaline-pumping descents to scenic cross-country routes, the region is a paradise for those who seek the rush of two wheels on rugged terrain. Discover the excitement of mountain biking in the Dolomites through these popular trails.

1. Sellaronda MTB Tour:
This iconic circuit takes you around the Sella massif, passing through four mountain passes and offering stunning views. The route is a mix of natural trails, gravel roads, and asphalt sections, making it suitable for intermediate to advanced riders.

2. Val Gardena Bike Day:
The Val Gardena Bike event is an annual event that opens selected trails for mountain biking enthusiasts. It features a variety of routes catering to different skill levels, allowing riders to explore the stunning Val Gardena scenery. The event is held

annually on the second Sunday of September, and it is open to cyclists of all levels. There are two routes to choose from: a shorter route of 15 miles and a longer route of 20 miles. If you are looking for a challenging and rewarding cycling experience, the Val Gardena Bike event is a great option.

You can register for the Val Gardena Bike event on the official website of the event: https://www.sellarondabikeday.com/en/.

3. Fassa Bike Park:
Located in the Val di Fassa, this bike park offers a variety of downhill and freeride trails suitable for experienced riders. With different levels of difficulty, it's a great place to challenge your skills and experience gravity-assisted fun.

4. Cortina d'Ampezzo Trails:
The Cortina area isn't just for winter sports; it also offers excellent mountain biking trails. From technical singletracks to leisurely rides, you can explore a range of terrains and landscapes.

5. Kronplatz:

Nestled amidst the majestic Dolomite peaks, the Kronplatz area is a haven for mountain biking enthusiasts seeking a blend of exhilarating trails and stunning alpine scenery. With a mix of downhill descents, cross-country routes, and accessible cable cars, Kronplatz caters to riders of all levels, promising an unforgettable biking adventure.

Mountain biking in the Dolomites offers an exhilarating way to explore the rugged terrain and stunning landscapes. Whether you're an experienced rider or a beginner, the variety of trails ensures that you'll find the perfect route for your biking adventure.

Rock Climbing Adventures

The Dolomites isn't just a visual masterpiece; it's also a rock climber's paradise. Towering limestone peaks and dramatic cliffs offer a diverse range of climbing experiences, from challenging multi-pitch routes to exhilarating via ferratas. If you're a climbing enthusiast, get ready to embark on an unforgettable rock climbing journey in the Dolomites.

1. Val di Fassa
Home to stunning rock walls, the Val di Fassa is a haven for climbers seeking challenging routes. Test your skills on multi-pitch classics, such as the "Oskar Schuster" route on the Pordoi Wall, and relish the sense of accomplishment at the summit.

2. Tre Cime di Lavaredo- The Iconic Three Peaks:
Among the most iconic features of the Dolomites, the Tre Cime di Lavaredo stands as not only a hiker's paradise but also a climber's dream. While renowned for their hiking trails, these majestic peaks offer

exhilarating climbing routes that provide a unique perspective on their towering beauty

3. Cinque Torri:

These five iconic towers are a magnet for climbers. The Cinque Torri area boasts a mix of single-pitch routes suitable for all levels, making it an ideal destination for both beginners and seasoned climbers. The unique formations and panoramic vistas add to the allure.

4. Sassolungo Group:

This iconic group of peaks offers not only breathtaking views but also exhilarating climbing opportunities. Choose from a variety of routes that cater to different levels of expertise and experience the rush of climbing against a backdrop of unparalleled natural beauty.

5. Catinaccio-Rosengarten Group:

With a blend of trad and sport climbing, the Catinaccio group offers a diverse range of routes amidst breathtaking alpine scenery. Whether you're ascending vertical faces or tackling overhangs, you'll be rewarded with awe-inspiring views.

6. Tofane: Dominating the landscape above Cortina d'Ampezzo, the Tofane group beckons climbers seeking multi-pitch challenges. Test your mettle on the renowned "Pompanin Route" on Tofana di Rozes; this is a must for experienced climbers.
As you ascend the granite walls, the panorama of the Dolomites' magnificence unfolds before you.

7. Civetta: Known as the "Aiguille of the Dolomites," Civetta offers a plethora of climbing routes that cater to various levels. The Via Ferrata degli Alleghesi is a classic climb that takes you up Civetta's imposing face. As you ascend the iron cables, soak in the sweeping vistas of the surrounding peaks and valleys.

Climbing in the Dolomites is a blend of physical challenge and breathtaking beauty. The sheer diversity of routes and the awe-inspiring landscapes will leave you with memories that last a lifetime. Whether you're a seasoned climber or just starting out, the Dolomites offer an unforgettable rock climbing experience. If you're a novice and want to explore, consider opting for climbing schools that offer guided experiences.

Adventure Sports

1. Paragliding and Hang Gliding: Soar like a bird and experience the Dolomites from a bird's-eye view with paragliding or hang gliding. Take off from strategic launch points such as Alpe di Siusi or Cortina d'Ampezzo and glide over the breathtaking landscapes, with the majestic mountains below and the open sky above.

2. Skiing and Snowboarding: In winter, the Dolomites transform into a winter wonderland, inviting skiers and snowboarders to hit the slopes. The region boasts extensive ski areas like the Dolomiti Superski, with over 1,200 kilometers of interconnected pistes. Revel in the world-class ski resorts of Alta Badia and Val Gardena, skiing through pristine powder against a postcard-perfect alpine backdrop.

3. Snowshoeing and Winter Hiking: For a more tranquil winter experience, explore the Dolomites on snowshoes or enjoy winter hiking on well-groomed trails. These activities provide a serene way to immerse yourself in the snowy landscapes of locations like Tre Cime di Lavaredo or Val di Funes, appreciating the peacefulness of the winter season.

4. Rafting and Canyoning: The Dolomites' rivers and canyons offer thrilling opportunities for rafting and canyoning adventures. Navigate the rushing waters and steep gorges under the guidance of expert guides in areas like the Avisio River or the Val di Sole, who ensure a safe and unforgettable experience.

5. Nordic Walking: Embrace the art of Nordic walking, a gentle and effective form of fitness that allows you to explore the Dolomites at your own pace. Follow the well-marked trails in locations like Alpe di Siusi or Val Gardena, and let the rhythmic motion of the poles guide you through the region's natural beauty.

CHAPTER 6: EXPERIENCING DOLOMITE CULTURE

Arts, Crafts, and Artisans

Immerse yourself in the world of artistry and creativity as we explore the rich tapestry of arts and crafts that thrive in this alpine wonderland. From intricate wood carvings to exquisite textiles, the work of Dolomite artisans reflects the region's cultural heritage and profound connection to the surrounding landscapes.

1. Woodcarving:

Woodcarving is a cherished art form in the Dolomites, and the skill of local woodcarvers is renowned far and wide. Wander through charming villages, and you'll discover exquisite wooden sculptures adorning balconies, facades, and churches. These intricate carvings often depict religious scenes, mythical creatures, and symbols of local traditions.

2. Textiles and Weaving:

Delve into the world of textile craftsmanship, where skilled weavers create intricate fabrics using traditional looms. The region's textiles are characterized by vibrant colors and intricate patterns, with each piece telling a story of its own. Explore local workshops and discover a wide range of textiles, including blankets, scarves, and traditional clothing.

3. Pottery and Ceramics:

Ceramics are an integral part of Dolomite culture, with potters skillfully shaping clay into utilitarian and decorative pieces. From sturdy cooking pots to delicate ornaments, each ceramic creation reflects the artistic vision of its maker. Take a pottery workshop, and try your hand at shaping the clay into your unique creation.

4. Painting and Art Galleries:

The Dolomites have inspired artists for centuries, and the region boasts numerous art galleries showcasing works of local painters and sculptors. The breathtaking landscapes and vibrant culture have served as muses for artists, resulting in an array of paintings and sculptures that capture the essence of the Dolomites.

5. Leatherworking:

Leatherworking is another craft deeply rooted in Dolomite tradition. Skilled artisans transform high-quality leather into exquisite belts, bags, shoes, and other accessories. Each piece is a testament to the artistry and attention to detail of the craftspeople.

6. Metalwork and Blacksmithing:

Metalwork and blacksmithing have been part of Dolomite culture since ancient times. Today, modern blacksmiths continue to create stunning metal sculptures and functional objects, showcasing the enduring appeal of this ancient craft.

7. Glassblowing:

The Dolomites are home to talented glassblowers who create delicate glass objects using traditional techniques. Visit a glassblowing studio, and witness the mesmerizing process of transforming molten glass into stunning artworks.

8. Workshops and Art Demonstrations:

Many artisans in the Dolomites welcome visitors to their workshops, where you can observe their creative process firsthand. Join an art demonstration, and gain insight into the techniques and passion behind these time-honored crafts.

By exploring the arts, crafts, and the work of skilled artisans in the Dolomites, you'll not only witness the region's cultural heritage but also become a part of its living history.

Dolomite's Festivals and Events

Throughout the year, the Dolomites come alive with a colorful tapestry of festivals and events that celebrate the region's rich cultural heritage and diverse traditions. These lively gatherings offer a unique opportunity to immerse yourself in the vibrant spirit of Dolomite culture and witness the locals' unbridled joy and sense of community. From ancient religious processions to contemporary music festivals, each event is a captivating reflection of the region's history, values, and zest for life.

1. Sagra dei Pastori (Shepherds' Festival):

Time of Year: Typically held in late June or early July, the Sagra dei Pastori pays homage to the region's shepherds and their flocks. Experience colorful parades, traditional music, and dancing as you witness the heartwarming bond between shepherds and their animals, showcasing their sheepdogs' remarkable herding skills.

2. Festa del Legno (Wood Festival):

Time of Year: Usually taking place in August, the Festa del Legno celebrates the art of woodcraft. Stroll through lively markets, and admire a diverse array of wooden sculptures, furniture, and traditional tools crafted by talented artisans.

3. Ferragosto:

Time of Year: Celebrated on August 15th, Ferragosto marks the peak of the summer season in the Dolomites. Join the locals for festive gatherings, concerts, and firework displays that light up the night sky, creating an atmosphere of joy and togetherness.

4. Notte delle Streghe (Night of the Witches):

Time of Year: Celebrated on the summer solstice, usually around June 21st, the Notte delle Streghe delves into the mystical world of folklore and legends. Locals dressed in traditional costumes reenact ancient stories of witches and magical beings, filling the night with enchantment and mystery.

5. Festa di San Vigilio (St. Vigilius Festival):

Time of Year: Held in early June, the Festa di San Vigilio honors the patron saint of the Dolomites. Processions, religious ceremonies, and traditional music pay tribute to the region's spiritual heritage, providing a glimpse into the profound reverence the locals hold for their religious traditions.

6. Bolzano Christmas Market:

Time of Year: Occurring during the Christmas season, starting from late November to early January, the Bolzano Christmas Market is one of the most famous Christmas markets in Italy. Adorned with twinkling lights and festive decorations, this market offers a delightful array of handcrafted gifts, local delicacies, and the joyful melodies of Christmas carolers.

7. Dolomiti Balloon Festival:

Time of Year: Held in January, the Dolomiti Balloon Festival is a magical event where colorful hot air balloons take to the skies against the backdrop of the majestic peaks. Witness the breathtaking beauty of the Dolomites from above as the balloons gracefully float through the alpine landscape.

8. Music Festivals:

Time of Year: Various music festivals take place throughout the year, with some occurring during the summer months and others during specific dates in the calendar. These festivals showcase a diverse range of musical genres and performances, offering a rich cultural experience.

Please note that festival dates can vary from year to year, so it's always best to check local event calendars and tourist information for the most up-to-date schedule when planning your visit to the Dolomites.

Participating in Dolomite's festivals and events allows you to embrace the region's cultural legacy and become part of the vibrant tapestry of its traditions. Each festival is a celebration of the Dolomites' soul, offering an opportunity to connect with the local communities and experience the joyous rhythm of life in this extraordinary alpine wonderland.

Folklore and Local Legends

In the heart of the Dolomites, unfolds a rich tapestry of folklore and local legends that have been passed down through generations. These captivating stories provide a glimpse into the region's cultural identity and the profound connection between the people and their stunning natural surroundings. As you explore the Dolomites, allow yourself to be transported into a world of enchantment and mystery, where ancient tales come to life

1. The Pale Mountains and the Enrosadira:

Among the most renowned legends of the Dolomites is that of the "Pale Mountains." According to local lore, the rosy glow that bathes the rocky peaks during sunrise and sunset, known as the Enrosadira, is a result of a curse placed on a powerful fairy queen. She cursed the mountains to blush in shades of pink and purple each day as the sun bid them farewell, ensuring that her beloved kingdom's beauty would forever be admired. Witnessing this ethereal display, I felt as if I had stepped into a fairy tale of my own.

2. The Kingdom of Fanes:

Deep within the heart of the Dolomites lies the mythical "Kingdom of Fanes," a hidden realm of ancient splendor. According to legend, the kingdom was inhabited by a proud and noble race, whose queen, Dolasilla, was renowned for her extraordinary beauty and wisdom. Yet, the Kingdom of Fanes vanished from the mortal world, fading into the mountains, and it is said that those with pure hearts might still catch a glimpse of its ethereal splendor on rare occasions.

3. The Dancing Witches of Sennes:

In the remote Sennes Valley, a tale of dancing witches captivates the imagination. witches from all corners of the Dolomites gather under the full moon in Sennes to revel and dance the night away. Their joyous celebration is said to bring good fortune to those who are fortunate enough to witness the enchanting spectacle.

4. The Legend of the Ciamorces:

Among the more haunting legends is that of the Ciamorces, mysterious creatures said to roam the Dolomite peaks. These nocturnal spirits take the form of white-clad figures, and their presence is both feared and revered. It is believed that encountering the Ciamorces during a mountain ascent might bring misfortune, yet some say they are protectors of the mountains, guiding travelers to safety.

5. The Dwarf Kingdom of Bula:

In the heart of the Dolomite forests lies the mystical realm of Bula, home to a diminutive race of dwarfs. Legend has it that these friendly beings are skilled guardians of the wilderness, tending to the flora and fauna with utmost care. Spotting a Bula dwarf is a rare privilege, and it is said that those who show respect and kindness might be granted the blessing of good fortune.

6. The Legend of the Furcheta Valley:

Deep within the Furcheta Valley, whispers of an ancient love story echo through the mountains. The tale speaks of a beautiful princess, Adèle, who fell in love with a young shepherd named Leonhard. Despite the challenges they faced, their love endured, and it is said that their spirits still roam the valley, entwined in eternal love.

As you explore the Dolomites, listening to these captivating tales and local legends, you'll come to understand that the mountains' allure goes beyond their breathtaking beauty. The stories woven into the very fabric of this enchanting land enrich your journey, adding a touch of magic and wonder to every step you take. Whether you encounter the dancing witches under the moonlight or catch a glimpse of the mythical Kingdom of Fanes, these legends will forever be etched in your heart, making your time in the Dolomites an unforgettable and enchanting experience.

Discover Popular Shopping Destinations

The Dolomites not only offer breathtaking landscapes and adventurous experiences but also a delightful shopping scene that caters to diverse tastes and preferences. From charming boutique shops to bustling markets, this section unveils the best shopping destinations that will leave you enchanted and with cherished souvenirs to remember your Dolomite journey.

1. Ortisei - A Shopper's Paradise:
Nestled in the heart of Val Gardena, Ortisei stands out as a haven for shoppers seeking traditional craftsmanship and unique gifts. Wander along the picturesque pedestrian streets, lined with artisan workshops and boutiques offering exquisite wood carvings, handcrafted ceramics, and intricately woven textiles. Whether you're looking for a one-of-a-kind souvenir or an artistic masterpiece to adorn your home, Ortisei will captivate you with its authentic Dolomite charm.

2. Bolzano's Piazza Walther - Cultural Treasures:

Bolzano's Piazza Walther is not only a bustling town square but also a shopper's delight. Surrounded by historic buildings and picturesque cafés, this vibrant square hosts regular markets, showcasing regional specialties and local handicrafts. Delight in sampling delectable South Tyrolean delicacies, like speck and artisanal cheeses, while perusing stalls brimming with handmade leather goods, intricate lacework, and contemporary art pieces.

3. Cortina d'Ampezzo - High-End Elegance:

Famed for its glamorous Alpine allure, Cortina d'Ampezzo offers a refined shopping experience where luxury meets tradition. Explore the chic boutiques along Corso Italia, where you'll find designer fashion, fine jewelry, and exquisite home decor. For those seeking unique treasures, visit local antique shops and art galleries, where authentic Dolomite artifacts and vintage finds await discerning shoppers.

4. Canazei - Mountainous Craftsmanship:

In the charming village of Canazei, shopping takes on a different tone as the Dolomite peaks provide a stunning backdrop to your retail excursions. Embrace the mountainous craftsmanship and peruse shops adorned with intricate lace, woolen garments, and wooden artifacts. Don't miss the opportunity to bring home some locally made honey, aromatic herbs, or a bottle of the region's renowned grappa to savor the flavors of the Dolomites long after your visit.

5. Selva di Val Gardena - A Paradise of Artistry:

Selva di Val Gardena, surrounded by majestic Dolomite peaks, is an idyllic destination to discover artistic treasures and unique souvenirs. Explore the town's artisan workshops, where skilled craftsmen produce awe-inspiring wooden sculptures and traditional hand-knitted garments. The artistry in Selva di Val Gardena extends to its jewelry boutiques, where expert goldsmiths create exquisite pieces inspired by the natural wonders of the region.

6. Belluno - Authentic Local Finds:

As the gateway to the Dolomites, Belluno offers a diverse shopping experience, reflecting the spirit of the region. Stroll through narrow cobblestone streets and uncover family-run stores that showcase a delightful array of local products, from handmade chocolates and artisan cheeses to traditional clothing and wooden crafts. Belluno's charming ambiance and authentic offerings make it a must-visit destination for shoppers seeking an authentic Dolomite experience.

When shopping in the Dolomites, keep an eye out for authentic locally-made products that showcase the region's rich cultural heritage and artistic flair. As you browse these popular shopping destinations, you'll find the perfect mementos to encapsulate the beauty and charm of your Dolomite adventure.

Cultural Etiquette and Customs

As you immerse yourself in the captivating Dolomite culture, understanding and respecting local customs and etiquette will enhance your overall experience and foster meaningful connections with the warm-hearted locals. The Dolomites are home to a rich tapestry of customs that reflect the region's deep-rooted traditions and values. Here are some cultural etiquette guidelines to help you navigate this enchanting world with grace and respect:

1. Greetings and Hospitality:
Dolomite locals take great pride in their warm hospitality and welcoming spirit. When meeting someone for the first time, a friendly handshake is common, and you may notice a warm embrace or two kisses on the cheek among acquaintances. When invited into a local's home or a mountain hut, accepting the gesture graciously allows you to savor authentic experiences and forge genuine connections with the people who call the Dolomites home.

2. Language and Communication:

While Italian is the official language in the Dolomites, many locals also speak Ladin, a Romance language unique to this region. Learning a few basic Italian phrases and greetings will go a long way in fostering friendly interactions and showing appreciation for the local culture. The locals will often respond warmly to any effort you make to communicate in their language, even if it's just a simple "Buongiorno" (Good morning) or "Grazie" (Thank you).

3. Dress Code:

The Dolomites offer a blend of traditional alpine influences and modern style. When exploring towns and villages, casual and comfortable attire is generally suitable. For visits to churches or more formal occasions, you may want to dress modestly and avoid wearing beachwear or revealing clothing as a sign of respect.

4. Mealtime Customs:
Sharing a meal with locals is an opportunity to savor the delectable flavors of Dolomite cuisine while partaking in cherished customs. During traditional meals, it's customary to wait for the host to say "Buon appetito" (Enjoy your meal) before beginning to eat. Take time to engage in lively conversations and relish each course as meals are often enjoyed leisurely, celebrating the art of good food and camaraderie.

5. Tipping and Service Charges:
Tipping is not obligatory in the Dolomites, as a service charge is typically included in the bill. However, leaving a small gratuity to show appreciation for exceptional service is always welcomed and well-received.

6. Photography and Respect for Sacred Sites:
As you capture the beauty of the Dolomites through your lens, be mindful of local customs and respect the sanctity of religious sites and cultural landmarks. Always ask for permission before taking photos of

people, especially in more intimate settings, and refrain from using flash photography in churches or museums to preserve the delicate artwork and artifacts.

By embracing the cultural etiquette and customs of the Dolomites, you'll find yourself embraced by the warmth and authenticity of the local community. The profound connections and shared experiences that arise from your respectful interactions will undoubtedly add a special dimension to your journey through this extraordinary region.

CHAPTER 7:
BEYOND THE DOLOMITES

Day Trips and Excursions

While the Dolomites offer an abundance of natural beauty and cultural treasures, venturing beyond its majestic peaks opens up a world of even more exploration and adventure. Embark on exhilarating day trips and excursions to nearby destinations, each offering its own unique charm and allure. From historic towns steeped in tales of the past to serene lakes cradled by rolling hills, these experiences promise unforgettable moments that complement your Dolomite journey.

1. Tre Cime di Lavaredo:

Located just a short drive from the heart of the Dolomites, the Tre Cime di Lavaredo is an iconic natural wonder. These three distinctive peaks stand tall, forming an awe-inspiring backdrop that beckons adventurers from far and wide. Embark on a day trip to witness the breathtaking views from the Rifugio

Auronzo, a mountain hut perched at the base of the peaks. As you hike along the well-marked trails, take in the splendor of the surrounding landscape, and embrace the exhilaration of being immersed in nature's grandeur.

2. Cortina d'Ampezzo:

Known as the "Queen of the Dolomites," Cortina d'Ampezzo is a captivating town renowned for its elegance and alpine charm. A day trip to this picturesque destination offers a blend of cultural experiences and breathtaking vistas. Stroll along the vibrant Corso Italia, lined with boutique shops and cafes, and soak in the relaxed ambiance of the Piazza Venezia. For those seeking adventure, take a cable car ride to the soaring Mount Faloria, where panoramic views of the Dolomite range await.

3. Lake Braies (Lago di Braies):

A visit to the enchanting Lake Braies, often referred to as the "Pearl of the Dolomites," promises an idyllic day amidst serene beauty. Surrounded by emerald forests and the imposing peaks, the turquoise waters of the lake invite leisurely walks or tranquil boat rides. Hike along the lake's shores and let the peaceful atmosphere embrace your soul. Capture the reflection of the mountains mirrored on the surface of the water, creating a picture-perfect memory to cherish.

4. The Villages of the Val Gardena:

A journey to the charming villages of Val Gardena, such as Ortisei, Selva Val Gardena, and Santa Cristina, provides a glimpse into the Dolomite's cultural heritage. The wooden-carved sculptures adorning the facades of rustic buildings, the aroma of freshly baked bread from local bakeries, and the welcoming smiles of the villagers paint a picturesque scene of alpine life. Delight in the region's artisanal handicrafts, from woodcarving to handwoven textiles, and immerse yourself in the heartwarming traditions of these quaint settlements.

5. Lake Misurina and the Three Peaks of Lavaredo:

Venture to Lake Misurina, aptly known as the "Pearl of the Dolomite Lakes," for a mesmerizing encounter with nature's splendor. The lake's tranquil waters reflect the surrounding peaks, creating a captivating mirror effect that mesmerizes visitors. From here, embark on a guided excursion to explore the Three Peaks of Lavaredo, immersing yourself in the magnificence of these iconic geological formations.

6. The Belluno Dolomites National Park:

For nature enthusiasts seeking a pristine wilderness, a day trip to the Belluno Dolomites National Park is a must. Embrace the untouched beauty of alpine meadows, crystal-clear streams, and dense forests teeming with wildlife. Lace up your hiking boots and set off on a trail to discover hidden waterfalls, tranquil glacial lakes, and breathtaking panoramas that will leave you in awe of Mother Nature's artistry.

These day trips and excursions beyond the Dolomites offer an enticing glimpse into the diverse beauty of the surrounding region. Each destination is a testament to Italy's rich cultural heritage and the enchanting allure of the Alpine landscape. Whether you seek adventure, culture, or moments of tranquil serenity, these experiences will enrich your Dolomite journey, leaving you with cherished memories that linger long after your return home.

Exploring Nearby Regions

While the Dolomites stand as the crown jewel of northern Italy, the allure of the surrounding regions is equally captivating. Embark on a journey to explore the nearby areas, each offering its own distinct charm and character. From historic cities steeped in art and culture to verdant valleys adorned with picturesque vineyards, these neighboring regions beckon with the promise of new discoveries and enriching experiences.

1. Venetian Lagoon and Venice:

Just a few hours' drive from the Dolomites lies the ethereal beauty of Venice, a city built on water. Navigate the Venetian Lagoon on a traditional gondola, gliding past ornate palazzos and intricate bridges. Stroll through the enchanting streets of the historic city center, where every corner reveals architectural masterpieces and timeless art. Savor the flavors of Venetian cuisine and indulge in the romance and grandeur of this iconic destination.

2. South Tyrol and the Wine Road:

Travel southward to South Tyrol, an enchanting region known for its Alpine meadows and world-renowned vineyards. Meander along the Wine Road, a scenic route that winds through rolling hills adorned with picturesque vineyards and charming villages. Sample exquisite wines and indulge in the delectable cuisine, where traditional Alpine flavors meld with Mediterranean influences. The fusion of cultures and landscapes creates an unforgettable experience.

3. Verona and Shakespearean Romance:

Delve into the timeless romance of Verona, a city steeped in history and immortalized by Shakespeare's "Romeo and Juliet." Wander through the ancient streets adorned with elegant archways and Renaissance palaces. Visit the iconic Juliet's House and stand on the balcony where young love once flourished. Explore the magnificent Verona Arena, a Roman amphitheater hosting breathtaking operas and performances. Embrace the city's poetic ambiance and be transported to a bygone era.

4. Lake Garda and the Garda Trentino:

Discover the allure of Lake Garda, the largest lake in Italy, nestled amid the Lombardy, Veneto, and Trentino regions. The beauty of this pristine lake is complemented by the surrounding mountains and charming lakeside villages. Embrace the tranquility as you bask in the Mediterranean climate, perfect for water sports and leisurely boat cruises. Venture to the Garda Trentino area, where you can hike through olive groves and vineyards, immersing yourself in the region's natural splendor.

5. Trento and the Dolomites of Trentino:

Journey to Trento, a city rich in history and cultural heritage, located amidst the stunning Dolomites of Trentino. Explore the medieval streets and discover the city's historical landmarks, including the Buonconsiglio Castle and the Cathedral of Saint Vigilius. For outdoor enthusiasts, the Trentino region offers a paradise of hiking trails, mountain biking routes, and rock climbing opportunities in the embrace of the Dolomites.

6. The Fiemme and Fassa Valleys:

Nestled between the peaks of the Dolomites, the Fiemme and Fassa Valleys are a paradise for nature lovers and adventure seekers. Traverse through verdant forests, witness the grandeur of towering waterfalls, and experience the warm hospitality of the local communities. Whether you choose to explore the vibrant flora and fauna during the summer or embark on exhilarating winter sports in the snow-clad landscapes, these valleys promise an immersive encounter with nature.

Exploring these nearby regions offers an opportunity to unravel the diverse layers of Italy's cultural and natural tapestry. Each destination complements the Dolomites with its own distinctive character and experiences, leaving you with a profound appreciation for the richness and variety that the surrounding areas have to offer. As you venture beyond the Dolomites, embrace the exploration of these neighboring treasures and let them weave unforgettable memories into your travel journey.

Hidden Gems and Lesser-Known Spots

The Dolomites' iconic peaks draw travelers from far and wide, though there are hidden gems and lesser-known spots waiting to be discovered by the intrepid traveler. These off-the-beaten-path destinations offer a sense of exclusivity and a chance to escape the crowds, allowing you to forge a deeper connection with the untamed beauty of the surrounding landscape.

1. San Martino di Castrozza:

Tucked away in the eastern part of Trentino, San Martino di Castrozza is a quaint village surrounded by majestic peaks. This lesser-known gem offers a peaceful retreat for nature enthusiasts and hikers. As you explore the Pale di San Martino, one of the most beautiful mountain groups in the Dolomites, you'll be rewarded with awe-inspiring panoramas and a sense of serenity rarely found in more popular tourist spots.

2. Lagazuoi and Cinque Torri:

For history buffs and outdoor enthusiasts alike, Lagazuoi and Cinque Torri provide a glimpse into the region's past amidst stunning natural surroundings. Take a cable car to Lagazuoi and explore the trenches and tunnels of the Open-Air Museum, which offers a fascinating look into the harsh realities of World War I. Nearby, the rock formations of Cinque Torri offer a playground for climbers and hikers seeking a unique perspective of the Dolomite peaks.

3. **Lake Sorapis**:

Hidden among the Dolomites lies the emerald beauty of Lake Sorapis. Accessible through a moderate hike, this lesser-known gem rewards adventurers with striking turquoise waters framed by rugged cliffs and evergreen forests. Bask in the tranquility of the secluded lake and savor the moment in harmony with nature.

4. **Val di Funes (Villnöß Valley)**:

Nestled within the Isarco Valley, Val di Funes is a hidden paradise of alpine meadows and rustic villages. The iconic Church of St. Johann against the backdrop of the Odle Group is a postcard-worthy scene that embodies the essence of the Dolomites. Hike through the idyllic meadows and embrace the slower pace of life in this lesser-explored corner of the region.

5. Lavaredo Loop Trail:

For a unique perspective of the iconic Tre Cime di Lavaredo, venture beyond the typical viewpoints and hike the Lavaredo Loop Trail. This lesser-known path weaves its way through meadows, forests, and rocky terrain, offering a closer encounter with the magnificent peaks. With fewer crowds and a sense of solitude, this trail allows you to immerse yourself fully in the grandeur of the Tre Cime.

6. Passo Giau:

As one of the Dolomites' most scenic mountain passes, Passo Giau is a well-kept secret among avid cyclists and photographers. Traverse the winding road to reach this panoramic vantage point, where breathtaking vistas of the surrounding peaks stretch as far as the eye can see. Whether you're capturing the golden hues of sunrise or the soft pastels of sunset, Passo Giau promises a visual feast.

7. The Vajolet Towers:

For daring mountaineers, the Vajolet Towers present an irresistible challenge. These soaring peaks, crowned with five majestic towers, offer a breathtaking panorama of the surrounding landscape. A climb to the summit rewards adventurers with a sense of accomplishment and vistas that stretch as far as the eye can see.

8. Lago di Carezza (Carezza Lake):

Known as the "Rainbow Lake," Lago di Carezza is a true marvel of nature. Its emerald waters mirror the Dolomite peaks, creating a kaleidoscope of colors that dance with the changing light. Stroll along the lake's shores, embraced by the tranquil ambiance, and let the beauty of this hidden gem captivate your soul.

9. Civetta:

The lesser-known Civetta mountain range offers a peaceful retreat, away from the hustle and bustle.

Embark on hikes along the paths of the Great War, where remnants of historic fortifications tell tales of the past. Gaze in awe at the impressive south face of Civetta, known as the "Wall of the Crows," an iconic sight for mountaineers and nature enthusiasts alike.

10. Cansiglio Forest:
The Cansiglio Forest, a vast expanse of ancient woodland, invites exploration and wonder. Wander through its leafy trails, discovering hidden lakes and lush glades. The forest's quietude is interrupted only by the songs of birds and the whispering breeze, offering a sense of solace amidst nature's embrace.

These hidden gems and lesser-known spots paint a captivating portrait of the Dolomites' well-kept secrets. Embrace the sense of adventure and discovery as you venture into these intimate havens, where the Dolomite's charm reveals itself in its most unassuming and untouched form. Each of these treasured locations promises a unique encounter, leaving you with memories of serenity and a connection to the essence of the Dolomites.

CHAPTER 8:
VISITING THE DOLOMITES ON A BUDGET

In this chapter, I'm excited to provide you with practical tips and insights that will help you savor the beauty of the Dolomites without stretching your budget. From budget-friendly accommodations to savvy travel hacks, you'll discover that the Dolomites offer a treasure trove of affordable adventures waiting to be explored.

Traveling on a budget doesn't mean compromising on the awe-inspiring experiences that await in the Dolomites. Instead, it's about embracing a different kind of adventure—one that allows you to immerse yourself in the region's natural splendor, local culture, and unforgettable moments without overspending. Whether you're a backpacker seeking epic hikes or a budget-conscious traveler in search of authentic experiences, this chapter will guide you through the art of making the most of your Dolomite journey while keeping your wallet happy.

Budget Accommodation Options

When it comes to exploring the Dolomites on a budget, finding the right accommodation can significantly impact your overall travel expenses. Luckily, the region offers a diverse range of budget-friendly options that cater to different preferences and styles of travel. Whether you're a solo adventurer, a backpacking enthusiast, or a budget-conscious family, the Dolomites have something for everyone.

1. Mountain Huts and Refuges: For a truly immersive experience in the heart of the Dolomites, consider staying in one of the traditional mountain huts or refuges. These rustic accommodations not only offer breathtaking views but also provide a unique opportunity to connect with fellow travelers and outdoor enthusiasts. Recommended mountain huts include Rifugio Lagazuoi and Rifugio Fuciade,

both well-known for their warm hospitality and stunning alpine locations.

2. Cozy Bed and Breakfasts: Dolomites' quaint villages and towns are dotted with charming bed and breakfasts. Staying in these family-run establishments not only provides a warm and welcoming atmosphere but also offers a chance to experience the local culture firsthand. Consider staying at B&B Ciasa Roch, known for its cozy ambiance and delicious homemade breakfast, or Albergo Bucaneve, a delightful guesthouse nestled amidst the Dolomite peaks.

3. Affordable Hotels and Inns: Look out for budget-friendly hotels and inns that provide basic amenities without compromising on comfort. Many of these options are strategically located, allowing you to explore the surrounding attractions conveniently. Hotel Meublé Sella and Hotel Cesa Tyrol are two well-known establishments that offer comfortable rooms and great value for money.

4. Camping and RV Options: If you're an outdoor enthusiast, camping or traveling in an RV can be an excellent choice. The Dolomites boast numerous campgrounds amidst stunning natural settings, where you can enjoy a night under the starry skies. Camping Sass Dlacia and Camping Seiser Alm are popular options for those seeking an authentic camping experience in the heart of nature.

5. Hostels and Guesthouses: Solo travelers and backpackers will find an array of hostels and guesthouses throughout the region. These budget accommodations provide the perfect opportunity to meet like-minded travelers while keeping expenses at bay. The Dolomite Mountains Hostel and Ostello Dolomiti are well-regarded options for budget-conscious travelers seeking comfort and camaraderie.

6. Farm Stays: Immerse yourself in the authentic rural lifestyle by opting for a farm stay. These charming accommodations offer a unique glimpse into local traditions and often include homemade

meals with fresh produce. Agritur Ciasa Vedla and Maso Pertica are both popular farm stays where you can experience the charm of Dolomite farm life.

7. Shared Accommodations: For those seeking to cut costs further, consider shared accommodations or room rentals through platforms like Airbnb. Sharing a space with fellow travelers can lead to new friendships and shared experiences. Look for shared apartments or private rooms in charming villages to enhance your budget-friendly stay.

When choosing budget accommodation options, remember that simplicity doesn't mean sacrificing comfort or authenticity. The Dolomites' budget-friendly lodgings offer an opportunity to create cherished memories while savoring the stunning natural beauty that surrounds you. Embrace the spirit of adventure, make new friends, and let the Dolomites be your welcoming home away from home.

Affordable Dining Options

One of the joys of exploring the Dolomites is indulging in the delectable cuisine that reflects the region's rich cultural heritage. While dining in the Dolomites can be a culinary delight, it's essential to find budget-friendly options that allow you to savor the flavors without straining your wallet. Here are some fantastic and affordable dining choices to enjoy during your Dolomite journey:

1. Trattorias and Osterias: These traditional eateries offer hearty, authentic meals at reasonable prices. From mouthwatering pasta dishes to local specialties like hearty stews and polenta, trattorias and osterias are perfect for a satisfying and budget-friendly dining experience.

2. Pizza by the Slice: For a quick and delicious meal on the go, look out for pizzerias that sell pizza by the slice. Grab a slice of freshly baked pizza topped with local ingredients and enjoy an affordable and tasty treat.

3.Aperitivo Time: Many bars and cafes in the Dolomites offer aperitivo, a pre-dinner ritual where drinks are served with complimentary snacks. Take advantage of this tradition to enjoy a drink and sample some free nibbles before dinner.

4. Local Street Food: Keep an eye out for local street food vendors and food trucks that offer regional specialties at reasonable prices. From panini filled with flavorful ingredients to mouthwatering pastries, street food is a delightful and affordable option.

5.Lunch Specials: Consider having your main meal during lunchtime when many restaurants offer special lunch menus at lower prices than dinner options. Take advantage of these deals to enjoy a quality meal without the premium cost.

6.Self-Catering with Picnics: As you explore the stunning landscapes of the Dolomites, opt for self-catering picnics with local bread, cheese, cured meats, and fresh produce. Create your own gourmet picnic while surrounded by nature's beauty.

7.Local Markets: Visit local markets and food stalls where you can find fresh and affordable produce, artisanal products, and regional delicacies. Pack your own picnic or prepare simple meals using these market-fresh ingredients.

8. Gelato Delights: Treat yourself to Italy's famous gelato at gelaterias scattered throughout the Dolomites. Enjoy a scoop or two of delicious gelato without breaking the bank.

9. House Wine: When dining at restaurants, consider ordering the house wine, which is often more budget-friendly than bottled options. Savor a glass of local wine that pairs perfectly with your meal.

10. Family-Run Pensions: If you're staying at a family-run pension or bed and breakfast, inquire if they offer homemade meals. These meals often showcase authentic family recipes and can be a memorable and affordable dining experience.

By embracing these affordable dining options, you can relish the delightful tastes of the Dolomites without overspending. Enjoy the region's culinary treasures, immerse yourself in the local food culture, and make the most of your budget-friendly gastronomic journey through this captivating paradise.

Free or Low-Cost Attractions

The Dolomites, with their breathtaking landscapes and captivating natural wonders, offer a plethora of attractions that won't cost you a fortune. Exploring the region's free or low-cost attractions is an excellent way to immerse yourself in its beauty and culture without breaking the bank. Here are some delightful and budget-friendly activities that will leave you feeling reconnected with nature and the essence of the Dolomites:

1. Hiking Trails: The Dolomites boast an extensive network of hiking trails, many of which are free to access. Lace up your hiking boots and embark on

scenic walks that lead you to awe-inspiring vistas, crystal-clear lakes, and lush meadows.

2. Picnic Spots: Discover picturesque picnic spots surrounded by majestic mountains and serene lakes. Pack your own delicious picnic and spend a leisurely afternoon reconnecting with nature.

3. Local Festivals: Keep an eye out for local festivals and events that celebrate the region's culture and traditions. Experience the vibrant atmosphere, sample local cuisine, and participate in traditional activities without spending a fortune.

4. Stunning Viewpoints: Drive or hike to stunning viewpoints that offer panoramic vistas of the Dolomites' iconic peaks. Marvel at the beauty of nature from these vantage points without any entry fees.

5. Historic Villages: Wander through charming historic villages that exude old-world charm and enchantment. Stroll along cobbled streets, admire

quaint architecture, and experience the local way of life, all for free.

6. Lakes and Waterfalls: Visit the region's picturesque lakes and waterfalls, where you can relax by the tranquil waters or feel the mist of cascading falls, all without spending a dime.

7. Wildlife Watching: The Dolomites are home to a variety of wildlife, including chamois, ibex, and marmots. Keep your eyes peeled for these beautiful creatures as you explore the wilderness.

8. Cultural Sites: Discover ancient churches, chapels, and historical sites that offer a glimpse into the region's cultural heritage. Many of these sites can be visited free of charge.

9. Sunrise and Sunset: Witness the magical spectacle of sunrise and sunset over the Dolomites' peaks. Find a scenic spot to watch the sky light up with hues of pink and orange as the day begins and ends.

Transportation Savings

Traveling through the enchanting Dolomites doesn't have to be a strain on your budget, especially when it comes to transportation. With a few savvy strategies, you can save money while getting around the region comfortably and conveniently. Here are some practical transportation savings tips to help you make the most of your Dolomite adventure:

1.Public Transportation Passes: Look into the availability of regional or multi-day public transportation passes. These passes often provide unlimited access to buses and trains within a specified area or time frame, offering great value for money.

2. Carpooling: If you're traveling with friends or fellow travelers, consider carpooling to share transportation costs. It not only reduces expenses but also allows you to enjoy the company of like-minded explorers.

3. Rentals: If you plan to explore the Dolomites extensively, renting a car might be a cost-effective option, especially if you split the expenses with travel companions. Having a car also provides flexibility in visiting more remote destinations.

4. Biking: Embrace the eco-friendly and budget-friendly option of biking in the Dolomites. Many areas have well-maintained cycling paths that allow you to discover the region at your own pace while enjoying the fresh mountain air.

5. Shuttle Services: Some regions in the Dolomites offer shuttle services to popular tourist spots. These shuttle services are often reasonably priced and provide a convenient way to reach attractions without the hassle of driving.

6. Group Tours: Joining group tours for specific activities or excursions can be a cost-efficient way to experience certain attractions. Group rates often offer savings compared to individual bookings.

7. Walking and Hiking: Many points of interest in the Dolomites are accessible by foot. Opt for walking or hiking to nearby attractions, and you'll not only save money on transportation but also have the chance to connect more intimately with nature.

8. Plan Efficient Routes: Organize your daily itineraries in a way that minimizes unnecessary backtracking and reduces travel time. Efficient routes help save on fuel costs and allow you to make the most of each day.

9..Combine Activities: When planning your activities, group nearby attractions together to avoid extra trips. This tactic saves time, money, and energy, allowing you to experience more during your visit.

By applying these transportation savings tips, you can navigate the Dolomites with ease and keep your travel budget in check. Enjoy the freedom to explore this captivating alpine paradise while knowing you're making the most of your money-saving journey through this natural wonderland.

Money- saving Tips

Exploring the awe-inspiring Dolomites on a budget doesn't have to be a daunting task. With careful planning and a little insider knowledge, you can make the most of your trip while keeping your expenses in check. Here are some money saving tips to help you embark on an unforgettable journey without breaking the bank:

1. Plan in Advance: Research and plan your trip well ahead of time to take advantage of early bird discounts on accommodation, transportation, and activities. Booking in advance can save you significant money.

2.Travel During Off-Peak Seasons: Consider visiting the Dolomites during the shoulder seasons of spring and fall. Not only will you enjoy milder weather and fewer crowds, but you'll also find lower rates on accommodations and attractions.

3. Use Public Transportation: The Dolomites have an efficient network of buses and trains that can take you to many scenic spots. Opt for public transportation to save on rental car costs and parking fees.

4. Pack Light: Packing only the essentials can help you avoid excess baggage fees and make your travels more comfortable, especially if you plan to move around frequently.

5. Cook Your Own Meals: If your accommodation has kitchen facilities, consider preparing some of your meals using local ingredients from markets or grocery stores. It's a great way to taste authentic flavors while saving on restaurant expenses.

6. Opt for Picnics: Take advantage of the region's stunning landscapes and have a budget-friendly picnic amidst nature. Grab some local bread, cheese, and fresh produce to create a delightful meal with a view.

7. Explore Free Attractions: The Dolomites boast a myriad of breathtaking natural wonders that are completely free to explore. Hike the scenic trails, visit picturesque lakes, and bask in the beauty of the great outdoors.

8. Look for Combo Tickets: Many attractions offer combo tickets that bundle multiple experiences at a discounted price. Consider purchasing these packages to get more value for your money.

9. Stay in Budget Accommodations: Embrace the unique charm of budget accommodations like mountain huts, hostels, and guesthouses. These options not only save you money but also offer a chance to connect with fellow travelers.

10. Utilize Tourist Cards: Some regions in the Dolomites offer tourist cards that provide free or discounted access to public transport, museums, and attractions. Check with local tourism offices for available options.

11. Pack Reusable Water Bottles: Staying hydrated is essential, especially during outdoor activities. Carry a reusable water bottle to refill at public fountains and save on purchasing bottled water.

By following these money saving tips during your Journey, you can experience the region's natural wonders, immerse yourself in local culture, and create unforgettable memories without exceeding your budget. Remember, a little creativity and resourcefulness can lead to a truly enriching and affordable journey through the enchanting Dolomites.

CHAPTER 9: DURATION AND ITINERARY SUGGESTIONS

Short stay 3-Days Dolomites Itinerary

Embarking on a journey to the Dolomites promises an experience like no other, where alpine grandeur meets cultural charm, and breathtaking landscapes unfold before your eyes. For those seeking an unforgettable adventure that captures the essence of this enchanting region, a 3-day itinerary will whisk you through the Dolomites' highlights and hidden gems. Whether you're a nature enthusiast, a history buff, or an avid adventurer, this carefully crafted itinerary offers a perfect balance of discovery and exploration.

Day 1: Alpine Splendor and Cultural Treasures

- Arrive in the Dolomites and choose your base town—Corvara, Ortisei, or any other picturesque spot. Get ready to immerse yourself in the alpine wonderland.
- Take a cable car ride to the top of Seceda and be greeted by a jaw-dropping panorama of the Dolomite peaks stretching far and wide.

- Stroll through the vibrant meadows of Alpe di Siusi, where wildflowers dance in harmony with the rugged mountains.

- Embrace the local culture with a visit to a traditional mountain hut for an authentic taste of Tyrolean cuisine.

Day 2: Captivating Legends and Natural Wonders

- Explore the charming town of Brixen (Bressanone) with its medieval architecture and colorful facades. Don't miss the stunning Brixen Cathedral and its artistic treasures.

- Journey to the ethereal Lake Braies, often called the Pearl of the Dolomites. Glide on its emerald waters, surrounded by towering peaks and lush forests.
- Discover the captivating legends and stories surrounding the enchanting Lago di Carezza, known for its iridescent colors and mystic aura.

- End the day by witnessing a mesmerizing sunset from one of the Dolomite's scenic viewpoints.

Day 3: Alpine Adventures and Scenic Drives

- Begin your day with a thrilling hike to the iconic Tre Cime di Lavaredo. The majestic triple peaks stand tall against the sky, offering an awe-inspiring sight.

- Embark on a picturesque drive along the Great Dolomites Road, winding through breathtaking landscapes and photogenic spots like Passo Giau and Passo Falzarego.

- Explore the charming village of Cortina d'Ampezzo, a renowned ski resort exuding Italian elegance. Stroll through its elegant streets and savor an authentic espresso at a local café.
- Conclude your Dolomites adventure with a cable car ascent to Mount Faloria, where the panoramic views bid you farewell in spectacular fashion.

In just three days, this Dolomites adventure will immerse you in the beauty, culture, and adventure of this breathtaking alpine wonderland. Embrace the natural splendor, delve into the local traditions, and create lasting memories that will keep the Dolomites forever in your heart.

7-Days Dolomites Itinerary

Prepare for an unforgettable week of exploration as we delve deep into the heart of the Dolomites. This 7-day itinerary will lead you through a captivating journey, where each day offers a new adventure and a chance to bask in the splendor of this alpine paradise. From majestic peaks to charming villages, and from cultural treasures to outdoor escapades, let the Dolomites weave their magic around you.

Day 1: Arrival and Acquaintance

- Arrive in the Dolomites and settle into your chosen base town, where comfort and tranquility await. Allow yourself to get acquainted with the alpine surroundings and the warm hospitality of the locals.

- Take a leisurely stroll through the town's cobblestone streets, where charming boutiques and artisanal shops offer a glimpse into the region's traditional craftsmanship.

- Indulge in a delectable dinner at a local restaurant, savoring the flavors of regional delicacies.

Day 2: Alpine Lakes and Rugged Peaks

- Embark on an adventure to the iconic Tre Cime di Lavaredo, where the three towering peaks provide a magnificent backdrop for your hike.

- Discover the enchanting Lago di Sorapiss, with its crystalline waters reflecting the surrounding peaks like a mirror.

- As the sun sets, capture the golden hour at one of the Dolomites' stunning viewpoints, where the landscape is bathed in warm hues.

Day 3: Cultural Gems and Historic Sites

- Explore the charming town of Bolzano, known for its blend of Italian and Austrian influences. Visit the South Tyrol Museum of Archaeology, home to Ötzi the Iceman, an ancient mummy dating back thousands of years.

- Wander through the ancient alleys of Brixen (Bressanone), where the imposing Brixen Cathedral and quaint squares offer glimpses into the past.

- Delight in the traditional flavors of Tyrolean cuisine at a local eatery.

Day 4: Enchanting Castles and Legends

- Venture to the fairytale-like Castle of Neuschwanstein, perched on a hill overlooking lush valleys and snow-capped mountains.

- Discover the legendary Lago di Carezza, also known as the Rainbow Lake, where local folklore comes alive with tales of love and magic.

- Relax in the evening at a spa or wellness center, indulging in moments of rejuvenation.

Day 5: Serene Valleys and Hidden Sanctuaries

- Explore the peaceful Val di Funes, where picturesque villages are nestled amidst lush meadows and imposing peaks.
- Visit the stunning Santa Maddalena Church, framed by the grandeur of the Dolomites, creating an idyllic setting.
- Take a scenic drive through the winding roads of Val Gardena, reveling in the breathtaking vistas along the way.

Day 6: Adventure in the Great Outdoors

- Embrace a day of outdoor adventures with options for rock climbing, paragliding, or mountain biking, suited to your preferences and skill level.
- Alternatively, set out on a rewarding hike to the pristine Alpe di Siusi, where the beauty of nature unfolds at every step.
- End the day with a well-deserved feast of regional dishes, celebrating the bounty of the Dolomites.

Day 7: Farewell and Fond Memories

- Before bidding farewell to the Dolomites, take a scenic drive through the Great Dolomites Road, savoring one last glimpse of the region's majestic landscapes.
- Reflect on your unforgettable journey as you enjoy a final meal in the heart of the Dolomites.
- Depart with cherished memories and the promise to return to this enchanting alpine wonderland.

Family- Friendly Activities Itinerary

Family vacations in the Dolomites are an opportunity for unforgettable bonding experiences amidst nature's wonders. If you're traveling with little adventurers, this tailored itinerary ensures an enchanting experience that caters to the whole family. From exhilarating outdoor excursions to immersive cultural encounters, the Dolomites promise fun-filled days for everyone to enjoy

Day 1: Family-Friendly Outdoor Fun

- Start your family adventure with a leisurely walk around the tranquil Lago di Dobbiaco, where little ones can spot ducks and swans gliding on the calm waters.

- Head to the Gardena Adventure Park for thrilling zip-lining and rope courses that promise a day filled with laughter and excitement.

- Conclude the day with a visit to a local gelateria for a sweet treat that both young and old will relish.

Day 2: Wildlife Encounters and Nature Exploration

- Embark on an easy hike to the Alpe di Siusi, Europe's largest alpine meadow. Children will delight in the lush greenery, while parents revel in the breathtaking Dolomite backdrop.
- Visit the Dolomites Wildlife Park in the Puez-Odle Nature Park, where little nature enthusiasts can observe local animals up close.

- Enjoy a picnic in the meadows, savoring the fresh mountain air and the tranquility of nature.

Day 3: Enchanting Castles and Family Entertainment

- Journey to the Castle of Trostburg, a fascinating medieval fortress with tales of knights and princesses that will captivate young minds.

- Head to a family-friendly farm to experience life in the Dolomite countryside, learning about farming and tasting farm-fresh produce.

- Conclude your family adventure with an entertaining puppet show at a local theater, filled with traditional Dolomite stories and captivating performances.

Day 4: A World of Fairytales

- Take the Family and visit the charming Lago di Braies, where the emerald waters and surrounding forests evoke the enchanting world of fairytales.

- Take a leisurely boat ride on the lake, and let imaginations soar amidst the breathtaking scenery.

- Head to the Prato Piazza, a vast plateau nestled amidst majestic peaks, and embark on an easy hike suitable for children. The stunning landscapes offer a playground of exploration and discovery.

- Unwind in a family-friendly mountain lodge, enjoying delicious local treats and cozy ambiance.

Romantic Retreats and Honeymoon Escapes

Nestled amidst stunning landscapes, the Dolomites serve as an idyllic backdrop for a romantic getaway or honeymoon. Couples seeking moments of serenity, adventure, and intimacy will find an array of enchanting activities and experiences designed to ignite passion and create cherished memories.The This section provides a 3-day honeymoon-friendly itinerary crafted to create cherished moments.

Day 1: Romantic Beginnings

- Arrive in the Dolomites and settle into your cozy mountain chalet or a luxurious boutique hotel, where romance fills the air.
- Take a peaceful stroll through the quaint streets of Ortisei, hand in hand, exploring charming shops and indulging in gelato.
- Enjoy a candlelit dinner at a Michelin-starred restaurant, savoring a delectable blend of local and international flavors.

Day 2: Love in the Air

- Take to the skies with a romantic hot air balloon ride over the Dolomites. Witness the awe-inspiring landscapes from a new perspective as you soar hand in hand above the mountain peaks.
- Venture to the romantic village of Ortisei, known for its charming atmosphere and artisanal shops. Stroll hand in hand through its quaint streets, pausing for a romantic lunch at a local trattoria.
- Savor an intimate dinner at one of the region's gourmet restaurants, indulging in delectable dishes paired with fine Italian wines.

Day 3: Captivating Moments

- Admire the sunrise from a scenic viewpoint, where the first rays of light paint the Dolomites in a soft golden hue. This breathtaking experience sets the stage for an unforgettable day.
- Choose an exhilarating activity to bond and create memories together. Whether it's tandem paragliding, horseback riding, or a private helicopter tour, the Dolomites offer endless options for adventurous couples.

- As the sun sets, take a leisurely stroll through a charming village, and savor a romantic gelato or crepe from a local vendor.

Day 4: Scenic Escapades and Tranquility

- Take a cable car ride to Monte Pana for a breathtaking view of the Dolomites, basking in each other's company amid nature's grandeur.
- Relish a romantic picnic in the enchanting Vallunga, surrounded by lush forests and the tranquil ambiance of the Dolomites.
- Unwind with a couple's spa treatment, rejuvenating your senses and creating moments of relaxation and intimacy.

The Dolomites offer a world of enchantment and romance, where couples can embrace each other's company and celebrate their love amidst nature's most stunning landscapes. Whether you're seeking adventure or tranquility, the Dolomites present an array of options for creating an intimate and unforgettable experience with your loved one.

CHAPTER 10:
PRACTICAL TIPS AND SAFETY

Health and Safety -
Prioritizing Your Well-being

While exploring the breathtaking landscapes of the Dolomites, it's crucial to be mindful of your health and safety. Keep this health and safety tips in mind

- Altitude Awareness: The Dolomites are known for their high-altitude terrain, so be aware of the potential effects of altitude sickness. Allow yourself time to acclimatize, especially if you're planning strenuous activities at higher elevations.

- Weather Precautions: The weather in the mountains can be unpredictable, so always check the forecast before heading out. Dress in layers to adapt to changing conditions and be prepared for sudden changes in temperature.

- Hydration and Nutrition: Stay hydrated, especially during physical activities, as the mountain air can be dehydrating. Pack nutritious snacks to keep your energy levels up during your excursions.

- Sun Protection: The Dolomites enjoy abundant sunshine, so don't forget to wear sunscreen and sunglasses to protect yourself from harmful UV rays.

- Emergency Contacts: Familiarize yourself with emergency numbers and the locations of nearby medical facilities in case of any unforeseen situations.

Remember, the key to a safe and enjoyable experience in the Dolomites is being prepared and attentive to your well-being.

Travel Insurance

When embarking on any journey, including your adventure in the Dolomites, having comprehensive travel insurance is a crucial aspect of ensuring peace of mind and protection throughout your trip. Travel insurance offers a safety net that can be invaluable in unforeseen circumstances, providing you with financial security and support in times of need.

1. Coverage for Medical Emergencies:
Travel insurance typically includes coverage for medical emergencies, such as accidents or illnesses that may occur during your trip. This coverage ensures that you can seek medical attention and treatment without the burden of high medical costs. Additionally, it may include emergency medical evacuation, which can be essential in remote mountainous areas.

2. Trip Cancellation or Interruption:
Life is unpredictable, and sometimes plans may change unexpectedly. Travel insurance can safeguard your investment by providing

reimbursement for non-refundable trip expenses if you need to cancel or interrupt your journey due to covered reasons, such as illness, injury, or unforeseen events.

3. Baggage Loss or Delay:

Losing your luggage or experiencing delayed baggage can be a significant inconvenience. Travel insurance can offer coverage for baggage loss or delay, helping you replace essential items or cover additional expenses until your belongings are returned to you.

4. Trip Delay or Missed Connection:

If your trip is delayed due to circumstances beyond your control, such as flight cancellations or severe weather, travel insurance can provide compensation for additional expenses incurred, such as accommodation and meals.

5. Personal Liability:

Accidents happen, and travel insurance can offer personal liability coverage in case you cause damage to property or injure someone during your trip.

6. 24/7 Assistance Services:
Many travel insurance policies come with 24/7 emergency assistance services, allowing you to seek help and guidance from professionals at any time, no matter where you are in the world.

Before purchasing travel insurance, carefully review the policy to ensure it covers your specific needs and activities while traveling in the Dolomites. Consider factors such as the duration of your trip, planned activities, and any pre-existing medical conditions that may require additional coverage.

Know these, investing in travel insurance is a small price to pay for the peace of mind and security it offers, ensuring that your Dolomite adventure is memorable for all the right reasons.

Language and Communication

As you embark on your journey to the Dolomites, you'll be stepping into a captivating region where diverse cultures and languages intertwine. While Italian is the official language in the majority of the Dolomite area, you'll also encounter various local languages and dialects spoken by the residents.

Here are some language and communication tips to help you navigate your way through this linguistic tapestry:

1. Learn Basic Italian Phrases:
While many locals in popular tourist areas may speak English, learning a few basic Italian phrases can go a long way in showing respect for the local culture and enhancing your interactions. Simple greetings, "thank you" (grazie), "please" (per favore), and "excuse me" (scusi) will be appreciated by the locals and may lead to more meaningful encounters.

2. Embrace Gestures and Body Language:
Communication isn't just about words—it's also about gestures and body language. Italians are known for their expressive gestures, so don't be surprised if you find yourself engaging in animated conversations using hand movements and facial expressions.

3. Carry a Phrasebook or Translation App:
Having a pocket-sized phrasebook or a translation app on your smartphone can be a lifesaver when faced with language barriers. These tools will help you communicate essential information or ask for assistance in various situations.

4. Seek Language-Friendly Establishments:
In popular tourist destinations, you're likely to find many businesses and establishments with English-speaking staff. Look for signs or ask locals for recommendations to find places where language won't be a barrier.

5. Be Patient and Respectful:
When communicating with locals who may not speak English fluently, patience and respect are key. Speak slowly and clearly, and avoid raising your voice in case you're not understood. A smile and a friendly attitude can go a long way in overcoming any language obstacles.

6. Cultural Sensitivity:
Understanding the local customs and cultural norms will also enhance your communication experience. For instance, Italians appreciate a polite and warm approach when interacting with strangers.

While language differences can initially seem daunting, they also present an opportunity for cultural exchange and memorable experiences. Embrace the linguistic diversity of the Dolomites, and you'll find that genuine connections can be made through the universal language of kindness.

Useful Italian Phrases

As you embark on your Dolomite adventure, arming yourself with a few key phrases in the local language can elevate your travel experience and foster connections with the friendly locals. While Italian is the predominant language spoken in the region, you may also encounter other languages and dialects in different areas. Here are some useful Italian phrases to help you communicate and navigate your way through this enchanting landscape:

1. Hello: Ciao (chow)
2. Good morning: Buongiorno (bwon-jor-no)
3. Good evening: Buonasera (bwon-a-se-ra)
4. Goodbye: Arrivederci (a-ree-veh-der-chee)
5. Please: Per favore (per fa-vo-re)
6. Thank you: Grazie (gra-tzee-e)
7. Excuse me/pardon me: Scusi (skoo-zee)
8. Yes: Sì (see)
9. No: No (no)
10. I don't understand: Non capisco (non ka-pee-skoh)

11. Could you help me, please?: Potrebbe aiutarmi, per favore? (po-tre-be a-yu-tar-mee, per fa-vo-re)

12. Where is...?: Dove si trova...? (do-ve see tro-va)

13. How much is this?: Quanto costa questo? (kwanto kos-ta kwes-to)

14. I would like...: Vorrei... (vo-rrei)

15. Can you recommend a good restaurant?: Può consigliare un buon ristorante? (pwo kon-sig-lyah-re oon bwohn rees-to-ran-te)

16. Cheers!: Salute! (sa-loo-te)

17. Help!: Aiuto! (a-yoo-to)

Remember, the key to successful communication is not just the words, but the warmth and openness you bring to the conversation. Locals appreciate the effort you put into learning their language, no matter how basic it may be. So, don't be shy to use these phrases, and you'll find that they can open doors to memorable experiences and meaningful connections during your time in the Dolomites.

Money and Currency Exchange

Before embarking on your Dolomite journey, it's essential to have a good understanding of the local currency and how to manage your finances during your trip. The official currency used in Italy, including the Dolomites, is the Euro (€). Here are some practical tips to help you make the most of your money during your adventure:

1. Currency Exchange: Upon arrival in Italy, you can exchange your home currency for Euros at various locations, such as airports, banks, currency exchange offices, or even some hotels. While airports are convenient, they may offer less favorable rates, so it's wise to shop around for better options in town.

2. ATMs and Credit Cards: ATMs are readily available in most towns and cities in the Dolomites, providing an easy way to withdraw cash as needed. Major credit cards like Visa and MasterCard are widely accepted in hotels, restaurants, and shops. However, it's always a good idea to carry some cash

for small purchases or in case you visit places with limited card acceptance.

3. Inform Your Bank: Before your trip, notify your bank and credit card companies of your travel plans to avoid any issues with international transactions. Inform them of the countries you'll be visiting, along with your travel dates, to prevent unexpected card declines.

4. Exchange Rates and Fees: Keep an eye on exchange rates to get the best value for your money. Some banks may charge foreign transaction fees or ATM withdrawal fees, so inquire about these fees beforehand to minimize additional costs.

5. Currency Conversion Apps: Consider using currency conversion apps on your smartphone to stay informed about exchange rates and calculate expenses accurately.

6. Cash vs. Card: While cards are convenient, some smaller establishments in remote areas may only

accept cash. Therefore, it's wise to have a combination of both to ensure you can make purchases wherever you go.

7. Safety Measures: Keep your money and important documents secure while traveling. Consider using a money belt or a travel pouch to safeguard your valuables, especially in crowded areas.

By being financially savvy and well-prepared, you can enjoy a worry-free experience in the Dolomites while effectively managing your expenses. Remember to strike a balance between cash and card usage, and don't forget to enjoy the incredible moments that this captivating region has to offer.

CHAPTER 11: RESOURCES AND HELPFUL INFORMATION

Emergency Contacts -
Your Safety Net in the Dolomites

While the Dolomites offer breathtaking beauty and thrilling adventures, it's essential to be prepared for any unforeseen circumstances during your journey. Familiarizing yourself with emergency contacts can provide you with peace of mind and a safety net should you require assistance. Here are important emergency contacts that you should have readily available throughout your travels in the Dolomites:

1. **Emergency Services:** In case of a life-threatening situation or immediate danger, dial the European emergency number 112. This centralized number connects you to police, medical services, and fire departments, ensuring swift and coordinated assistance.

2. Local Police (Carabinieri): For non-emergency situations that require police intervention or reporting, reach out to the Carabinieri, Italy's military police, at 112 or their direct line at 112.

3. Medical Emergencies: In the event of a medical emergency, such as injuries or sudden illnesses, contact the local emergency medical services by dialing 118.

4. Mountain Rescue: If you're exploring the mountains and encounter difficulties or need rescue assistance, call the mountain rescue service at 118.

5. Consulates and Embassies: If you're a foreign traveler in need of consular assistance, locate the nearest embassy or consulate of your home country. They can provide support with lost passports, legal matters, or any other consular services.

6. Roadside Assistance: If you experience car trouble or require roadside assistance, dial the Automobile Club d'Italia (ACI) helpline at 116 for prompt help.

7. Poison Control: In the event of accidental poisoning or toxic exposure, contact the poison control center at 112 or the local health authority.

It's important to keep a list of these emergency contacts saved on your phone or written down in a secure location. Additionally, share your travel itinerary and accommodation details with a trusted friend or family member who can assist in case of emergencies.

While exploring the Dolomites is a thrilling adventure, being prepared for any emergency ensures a safe and enjoyable trip. With these essential emergency contacts at your fingertips, you can focus on embracing the wonders of the Dolomites with confidence and tranquility.

Local Tourism Offices and Contacts -

Your In-Person Guides to the Dolomites

While online travel websites and apps offer a wealth of information, there's nothing quite like the personalized assistance and local expertise provided by tourism offices in the Dolomites. These dedicated teams are passionate about their region and are eager to help you make the most of your time here. Whether you need recommendations for off-the-beaten-path attractions, advice on the best hiking trails, or insights into the region's rich culture, the local tourism offices are your go-to resource. Here's how to connect with them:

1. **Dolomite Tourism Office (Local Information Centers):** The Dolomites are scattered across multiple regions and provinces,

each with its own tourism office. These local information centers serve as a valuable resource for visitors, offering maps, brochures, and expert advice on the best things to see and do in their specific area. Don't hesitate to stop by one of these offices upon arriving in your chosen destination.

2. Val Gardena Tourism Office: Located in the picturesque Val Gardena valley, this tourism office specializes in providing information and assistance to visitors exploring this enchanting region. Whether you're interested in winter sports or summer adventures, the friendly staff will be delighted to guide you.

3. Alta Badia Tourism Office: Nestled in the heart of the Dolomites, Alta Badia is known for its breathtaking landscapes and rich cultural heritage. The local tourism office can help you plan your itinerary, recommend hiking routes, and share insights into the area's unique traditions.

4. Cortina d'Ampezzo Tourism Office: If you're heading to the stunning resort town of Cortina d'Ampezzo, the local tourism office is a great resource for discovering the best places to ski, hike, and indulge in delicious local cuisine.

5. Seiser Alm Tourism Office: As one of the largest high-altitude plateaus in Europe, Seiser Alm offers boundless natural beauty and outdoor activities. The tourism office can assist you with trail maps, information on guided hikes, and details on the region's cultural events.

6. Bolzano Tourist Information Office: In the vibrant city of Bolzano, the tourist information office can provide insights into the city's historical landmarks, shopping districts, and renowned museums.

Remember to check the opening hours of the tourism offices, especially during public holidays and off-peak seasons. These helpful contacts are eager to share their passion for the Dolomites and will ensure you have a memorable and rewarding experience exploring this captivating alpine wonderland

Recommended Tour Operators

Exploring the Dolomites can be an exhilarating journey, but to truly make the most of your experience, consider joining a guided tour with one of the region's reputable tour operators. These experts are well-versed in the area's natural wonders, cultural heritage, and thrilling activities. Whether you're a seasoned adventurer or a first-time visitor, a guided tour allows you to delve deeper into the hidden gems of the Dolomites. Here are some recommended tour operators to consider:

1. **Dolomite Mountains**: Specializing in tailored adventures, Dolomite Mountains offers a wide range of guided tours for all levels of experience. Whether you're interested in hiking, skiing, climbing, or biking, their knowledgeable guides will lead you to iconic landmarks and lesser-known spots, ensuring an unforgettable journey.

2. **Alpine Guide**: For those seeking an authentic mountaineering experience, Alpine Guide offers expert-guided expeditions, climbing courses, and

trekking tours in the Dolomites. Their certified mountain guides prioritize safety and sustainability, while also sharing their profound passion for the mountains.

3. ItalyTours.EU: If you're looking for a comprehensive Dolomite experience, ItalyTours.EU provides multi-day tours that combine the beauty of the Dolomites with visits to nearby regions like Venice and Verona. Their itineraries encompass cultural immersions and breathtaking natural wonders.

4. Dolomiti SkiRock: With a focus on winter adventures, Dolomiti SkiRock specializes in ski touring and snowshoeing excursions. Their seasoned guides will lead you through powder-filled landscapes and pristine winter trails, making your snowy escapades truly memorable.

5. DolomiteBiking: Mountain biking enthusiasts will delight in the guided tours offered by DolomiteBiking. From thrilling downhill descents to scenic cross-country routes, their experienced guides know the best trails for adrenaline-pumping rides.

6. Walks Inside Nature: For a unique perspective on the Dolomites, Walks Inside Nature offers guided tours that emphasize mindfulness and connection with nature. With a focus on slow travel and eco-friendly practices, these tours allow you to savor every moment of your journey.

7. Intrepid Travel offers a variety of group tours in the Dolomites, including hiking, biking, and skiing.

8. Exodus Travels is another company that offers group tours in the Dolomites. They specialize in active travel, so their tours are perfect for those who want to get out and explore the mountains.

Before choosing a tour operator, take the time to read reviews and testimonials from fellow travelers to ensure they align with your interests and values. Each tour operator has its own specialty, so whether you're seeking an adrenaline-filled adventure or a leisurely cultural exploration, there's a guided tour that's perfect for you. Embrace the expertise of these tour operators, and let them unlock the full potential of your Dolomite experience.

Useful Websites, Maps, Apps

Your Guide to Navigating the Dolomites

As you prepare for your unforgettable journey through the Dolomites, arming yourself with valuable resources will enhance your travel experience and ensure a seamless exploration of this stunning Mountainous wonderland. Here are some useful websites, maps, and apps that will be your trusted companions during your adventure:.

1. Dolomites Tourism Websites: The official tourism websites of the Dolomite regions provide a wealth of information, including travel guides, event calendars, accommodation listings, and suggested itineraries. Some reliable websites include Dolomites Val Gardena, Visit Dolomites, and Dolomiti.org.

2. Offline Maps: Before setting off on your exploration, download offline maps of the Dolomites to your smartphone or tablet. Apps like Google Maps, Maps.me, and Komoot offer detailed offline

maps that can help you navigate even in areas with limited internet connectivity.

3. Dolomiti Superski: If you're planning to hit the slopes during the winter season, the Dolomiti Superski app is a must-have. It's a valuable companion. It provides an interactive map of the vast ski area of Dolomite, snow conditions, lift status, and ski pass options, ensuring you make the most of your time on the slopes.

4. Dolomite Experience (App): This app offers a range of digital tours, audio guides, and interactive maps to enhance your experience of the Dolomites' cultural and natural wonders.

4. Trekking Apps: For avid hikers, apps like AllTrails, ViewRanger, and Wikiloc offer an extensive collection of hiking trails, complete with detailed descriptions, difficulty levels, and user reviews.

5. Weather Forecasts: Stay updated on weather conditions in the Dolomites by using reliable weather forecast apps such as AccuWeather, Weather.com, or Yr.no.

6. Public Transportation Apps: If you plan to utilize public transportation to get around, consider using apps like Südtirol2Go or DolomitiMobilCard to access bus and train schedules in the region.

7. Travel Forums and Blogs: Connect with fellow travelers and gain valuable insights by exploring online travel forums like TripAdvisor.

Before and during your trip, these resources will serve as indispensable tools to help you plan your activities, navigate the terrain, and fully immerse yourself in the wonders of the Dolomites. Whether you're seeking hiking trails, local events, or the best dining spots, these websites, maps, and apps will be your companions on this enchanting journey.

Conclusion

As we come to the end of this travel guide, I hope you feel inspired and excited to embark on your own unforgettable journey through the breathtaking Dolomites. This enchanting region, nestled in the heart of the Italian Alps, beckons with its awe-inspiring landscapes, rich cultural heritage, and boundless adventure opportunities.

Throughout this guide, we've explored the many facets that make the Dolomites a world-class destination. While words and images can paint a vivid picture of the Dolomites, there's truly no substitute for experiencing it in person. Each day spent in this alpine paradise will leave an indelible mark on your heart, and every step taken on its trails will leave you in awe of nature's grandeur.

Don't forget to venture beyond the well-trodden paths and explore the hidden gems and lesser-known spots that the Dolomites guard with loving secrecy. And as you immerse yourself in the wonders of nature, remember to respect the fragile environment and leave only footprints behind.

Whether you're traversing the trails on a family vacation, embarking on a thrilling solo adventure, or embarking on a romantic honeymoon, the Dolomites will capture your heart and soul in ways you never imagined.

As you venture through the Dolomites, I wish you unforgettable moments, new friendships, and a profound appreciation for the wonders of our world. Embrace every second of this journey, for the Dolomites have a way of leaving an indelible mark on those who seek their beauty.

So, with your guidebook in hand, your heart filled with excitement, and your spirit of adventure ignited, I encourage you to embark on this remarkable odyssey through the Dolomites. May your travels be safe, your memories be treasured, and your soul forever be touched by the splendor of the Dolomites.

Bon voyage, May your Dolomite journey be an unparalleled celebration of life and nature.

Made in the USA
Las Vegas, NV
11 October 2023